James Whale:
A Biography
or
The Would-be Gentleman

Mark Gatiss

CASSELL

For Terry Bolas
Constant friend and inspiration
With love

Cassell
Wellington House
125 Strand
London WC2R 0BB

215 Park Avenue South
New York
NY 10003

First published 1995

British Library Cataloguing-in-Publication Data
A catalogue record for this book is available from the British
Library.

ISBN 0–304–32863–4 (hardback)   1000524707
    0–304–32861–8 (paperback)

Excerpts from R.C. Sherriff's *No Leading Lady* (London: Gollancz,
1968) reproduced with permission of Curtis Brown.

Typeset by York House Typographic Ltd
Printed and bound in Great Britain by
Biddles Ltd, Guildford and King's Lynn

Contents

Preface

LIKE many others, I first became aware of James Whale through the quartet of horror films he made for Universal Studios in the 1930s. Frequently shown in television double bills, the films of this period were a staple of my childhood, but I remember finding most of them creaky and dull, something to be endured rather than enjoyed until the Eastmancolor glory of a Hammer picture later in the evening.

Whale's films, however, always struck me as different. The starkness of *Frankenstein*, the blackly comic nastiness of *The Invisible Man* and, in particular, the sheer bizarreness of *Bride of Frankenstein* spoke of an unusual talent at work and, I fervently believed, a kindred spirit.

As I grew older and sharpened my critical faculties, Whale's work grew even larger in stature. Tod Browning's *Dracula*, while undeniably popular in its day, appeared turgid and stagey, while Whale's *Frankenstein* is unquestionably the finest version of the now oft-told story. *Bride of Frankenstein*, a symphony of the grotesque, goes even further and presents, in Ernest Thesiger's Dr Pretorius, one of the screen's most gloriously camp and obvious homosexuals. It is this camp sensibility, combined with a streak of cynical and sometimes genuinely unsettling humour, which most attracted me to Whale's work and, ultimately, to the man himself.

I knew he had directed a version of *The Man in the Iron Mask*, and this seemed an entirely logical progression for such a flamboyant film-maker. It was only when I saw the 1936 *Showboat* and discovered to my astonishment the credit 'A James Whale Production' that an extra dimension to his work began to show itself. Surely this couldn't be James Whale 'the horror man'? My interest was further aroused by revelations in Kenneth Anger's

Hollywood Babylon that Whale had been outrageously indiscreet, a hedonist who 'enjoyed the sight of young men in bathing trunks', a man eventually brought down by a homophobic film industry. Somewhere within this lurid myth, I suspected, lay the truth.

Over the years, thanks to the tireless research of writers such as Gregory Mank and particularly James Curtis, a fuller picture was revealed. James Whale had directed both stage and screen versions of R C Sherriff's *Journey's End*, an early treatment of *Waterloo Bridge* and a sequel to *All Quiet on the Western Front* called *The Road Rack*. In addition there was a wonderful screwball comedy, *Remember Last Night?*, Galsworthy's *One More River* and even a jungle adventure, *Green Hell*. The discovery of his lost classic *The Old Dark House* provided the icing on the cake. Clearly there was a great deal more to this man than had first appeared.

What I missed, however, in all the established research on Whale was any real acknowledgement of his sexuality: a fundamental fact which, to me, was mutually indivisible from his life and art. I wanted to find the truth behind the popular picture of 'the Queen of Hollywood'. It was no easy task. Researching this book became a story in itself; good luck, coincidence and detection combined in equal measures. Whale seems a determinedly unknowable figure. Self-effacing and extremely reserved, it is very hard to form a fully rounded picture of him. What was really going on beneath that slim and exquisitely dressed façade? There are no recordings of his voice, only a modest scattering of newspaper interviews and precious few people surviving who knew him well. Various accounts paint him as arrogant and cold, others as warm, generous and witty. It is as if Whale were cocking an amused eyebrow at us from beneath the smoke of his trade-mark cigars. The picture that finally emerged has both surprised and delighted me, proving far more interesting than the superficially attractive campness of *Hollywood Babylon*'s original lure.

James Whale was an extraordinary man, virtually the only British director working in Hollywood during one of its most influential periods, and one of the few never to make a film in his own country. His success lasted only a short time, yet he managed to make his mark in more genres than he is ever given credit for. Most interesting of all, though, James Whale was a man who coped far better with his homosexuality than with his working-class origins. While he quite happily flouted accepted sexual convention, he strove all his life to reinvent himself as a gentleman. It is this sense of determination, of struggle against the injustice of the British class system, of a man who always strove to be *in control* which shouts through the silence of Whale's wilful obscurity.

'No, not *that* one' is the most frequent response I have made to enquiries during this book's long gestation. It is indeed unfortunate that my subject should share his name with the host of a late-night British television show, but it is an irony which would probably have pleased James Whale immeasurably.

Mark Gatiss
London, 1995

Acknowledgements

GREGORY William Mank who kindly allowed me access both to his published material and interviews with Mae Clarke, Douglas Fairbanks Jnr, Zita Johann, Valerie Hobson, Alan Napier, Elsa Lanchester, Gloria Stuart, Shirley Ulmer and Marilyn Wood.

Joss Ackland, Forrest J Ackerman, Peter Barnsley, Stephen Bourne, Simon Callow, David Chierechetti, Constance Cummings, Ned Comstock of the University of Southern California, the late Peter Cushing, Sir John Gielgud, William E Guthner, Curtis Harrington, Austin and Howard Mews, Harry Morgan, Ken Sefton, Gloria Stuart, Jane Wyatt and all at the Margaret Herrick Library, Los Angeles.

Particular thanks go to: John Abbott (glorious memories, friendship and a true Hollywood welcome); James Curtis (kindness and good grace); and Pierre Foegel (for letting me put a few things straight).

Chapter one

IT was into the unpromisingly bleak landscape of Dudley, Worcestershire, that James Whale was born on 22 July 1889. Dudley was a small but thriving industrial community of under sixty thousand people which had grown up around the mound of its famous medieval castle. By the time of Whale's birth, it was as grim and soot-blackened as any boom town of the late nineteenth century.

James was the sixth of seven children born to William Whale, a blast-furnaceman, and his wife Sarah in their little house at 41, Brewery Street in the Kate's Hill district of the town. A further three children died in infancy. Practising Christians, the family were regular worshippers at Dixon's Green Methodist Church. Their neighbour Cyril Turner, who at that time lived with his grandparents at number 43, vividly recalled the Whales and their generosity. William Whale kept pigs at the bottom of the rear garden and, after he had killed one, it was young Cyril's job to take the offal and joints of meat to all the neighbours in the street. The Whales practised what they preached, endeavouring to help their fellow men wherever possible.

'Behind the pig-sty was a row of very tall trees which would make a strange sound as the wind moaned through them. I can still hear that eerie sound now.'[1]

As well as his connections in church-based social work, Whale senior was also prominent in union activities, becoming local secretary of the ironworkers' union he had helped to establish.

Young James went to Bayliss's School in Tower Street and then to the imposing Dudley Bluecoat School, which survives to this day. He was already showing some talent as an artist and had earned himself extra pocket money writing out price tags in immaculate lettering for local shopkeepers. Thin, redheaded, detached and shy, Whale was clearly different from his fellows from the very beginning. He hated the manual labour which seemed to be his only destiny and longed for an avenue of escape from the depressing landscape of the Black Country. His strong religious upbringing and the ugliness of his surroundings left an indelible mark on the sensitive young man, as his friend Elsa Lanchester would recall: 'He came from a poverty-stricken English family, and I had heard him describe the tiny little fire in the tiny little grate in the rooms where he was brought up.'[2]

For a while, James worked in a cobbler's shop in Eve Hill before taking a job embossing patterns onto fenders at the factory of Harper and Bean in Waddham's Pool. He disliked the work intensely but could not afford to give it up. Poverty also precluded the possibility of a proper four-year course in art which would have provided him with the necessary qualifications. His only choice was to enrol as an evening student at the Dudley School of Arts and Crafts, which he did in 1910. Whether he ultimately intended to teach or not is unsure.

A contemporary, John Hadley Rowe, had marked the young James's manner as 'distinctive' even as a schoolboy, though he only knew him then by sight. Later to become Vice-principal of St Martin's School of Art, Charing Cross Road, Rowe spoke to historian Peter Barnsley about his reserved friend. 'Whale looked and behaved like a gentleman,' concluded Barnsley, 'and kept himself a little apart, though he was by no means aloof. He had an artist's introspection and chose his company to suit himself.'[3] Thus, a familiar, if hackneyed picture of homosexual inclination is already in evidence: a reserved boy who seemed 'different', seeking escape from a grim reality through his art.

At the evening classes, John Hadley Rowe and Whale soon became firm friends and would spend summer weekends on sketching trips, travelling to Dudley Castle, the Fox Yards or 'Wren's Nest', a sizeable quarry which is now a protected site of geological interest. After a while, Whale bought a 'Matchless' motor cycle and the two friends would ride out to Wombourn Common to draw and paint. It was during these trips that the first indication of Whale's interest in the theatre showed itself. Rowe recalled that

Whale was a brilliant mimic and would entertain him with hilarious impersonations of friends. More often, though, Whale would study the characters in the melodramas he and Rowe attended at the Dudley Opera House. These visits began because Rowe's father displayed the theatre bills in the windows of his business, 'The Two Bulls' Heads' in Stone Street, and was given tickets for the shows. It was Whale and Rowe, however, who took advantage of the free gifts, experiencing such delights as *Alone in London*, *The Span of Life* and *The Face at the Window*. Apparently, Rowe did not detect in his friend any particular inclination towards a career in the theatre; simply that his artistic temperament took in a broad range of interests.

As for Whale's most pronounced talent at that time, John Rowe had great admiration:

> His outlook on drawing was unusual, because he had a pronounced sense of selection for essential characteristics. His portrait drawings, which were many, varied considerably by the skilful change in technical methods suggested by the personality of the subject. I well remember his wash drawing of a Bluecoat School boy complete with chequered cap band and ribbon, being resolved magnificently in indigo blue; a result which would startle students even now at the Royal Academy schools or the Slade.[4]

Obviously talented, Whale was frustrated by the opportunities his low birth presented him, as his friend Alan Napier recalled: 'He had been a skinny, slightly undersized kid ... With his artistic talents and ambitions, he was a fish out of water. He had a dream.'[5] Whale began first to educate himself and then to alter his speech, eliminating the strong Black Country accent in favour of a clipped, upper-class tone. As gifted a mimic as he was, it took patience and time to effect the transformation. James Whale, the Dudley artisan, was disappearing. Whale's dream was to become an English gentleman.

With a career in the arts apparently blocked, he began to look about for some other means of escape. This arrived in the unlikely form of the First World War which broke out when Whale was twenty-five. Neither Whale nor John Rowe were particularly keen to join up, and Rowe freely admitted that it was only the constant shower of white feathers which persuaded him to join the navy. For his part, Whale spent a short time working for the YMCA in Whittington barracks, Lichfield and then, in October 1915, enlisted in the Inns of Court regiment as an officer cadet. Whale's commission was no mean feat for the son of a Dudley furnaceman, even allowing for the tremendously high casualty rate among junior officers on the Western Front. The life expectancy of a subaltern was three weeks. In the late summer of 1916, Whale joined the 2nd battalion of the 7th Worcestershire regiment in France as a second lieutenant, serving on the Somme, and at Arras and Ypres.

There are scant details concerning Whale's experiences in the war, though he would bring his intimate knowledge of dugout life to his design and direction of R C Sherriff's *Journey's End* some years later. He was always a modest man and inclined to make light of the time he spent in action. As a conservative patriot, he would have approached the fight against the Kaiser's forces as a simple duty, viewing the suffering, boredom and distress as things to be borne with dignity. By becoming a commissioned officer, Whale took a further step towards his goal of becoming an English gentleman. Furthermore, the war presented the chance to escape from Dudley and see something of the world, albeit under very trying circumstances. It would also have given him his first experience of close contact with other men and, in all probability, his sexuality.

On 25–26 August 1917, Whale led his men to an advance on the Pommern Redoubt, in Belgium. The attack was driven back with heavy losses and Whale was captured:

> My platoon had been told off to do a stunt on a pill-box at midnight and we had gone into a well-laid trap. It all happened so suddenly I was stupefied and found it impossible to believe myself cut off from everything British and in the hands of the Huns.[6]

Whale's incarceration, first in a camp in Karlsruhe, then in Holsminden near Hanover, proved to be the first real turning-point in his life. At the camp, he became heavily involved in amateur dramatics. Bored and frustrated, the prisoners had developed their dramatic efforts to a highly professional standard, employing elaborate stage effects and specially ordered costumes from Cologne! A man of Whale's talents was highly prized and, in addition to performing for the first time, he made literally hundreds of line and wash drawings for the shows. He spent fifteen months in the camp with 1400 other men before being repatriated. However, the war, and particularly his experiences in the camp had changed Whale for ever. The theatre would be his route to peace-time freedom.

Back in England, Whale sold some of his prison-camp sketches to *The Bystander* magazine, and was soon after taken on as staff cartoonist. With the money he made from this job he began to seek employment in the professional theatre. Barry Jackson's Birmingham Repertory Company, already nationally famous and only a few miles from Dudley, seemed an obvious starting-point. Jackson recalled that Whale was a constant backstage visitor, craving employment, until he was finally taken in. Whale spent most of his eighteen months at the Rep with their touring production of John Drinkwater's *Abraham Lincoln*. As well as designing the set, Whale was a stage-manager and played a number of small roles. Although occasionally called upon to play Booth himself, Whale's regular role was that of an orderly whose only line was 'A dispatch, sir'. Determined to make an impression, he changed the inflection of the line for every performance.

Whale's stage debut proper came on 30 August 1919 in Barry Jackson's production of Beaumont's *The Knight of the Burning Pestle* (?1607). Whale played only a small part, but was emboldened by a determination to succeed in his new profession. Later that year he travelled north for another supernumerary part, this time in Shakespeare. It was here that he met the man who was to become a lifelong friend, Ernest Thesiger. 'I first met James Whale in 1919 when, as a frail ex-prisoner of war with fawn-like charm, he played a small part in a Christmas production of *The Merry Wives of Windsor* in Manchester.'[7]

Whale's friendship with Thesiger was delightful and fruitful, the two men enjoying each other's company hugely. Whale was never flamboyant about *his* homosexuality, but probably found in

Thesiger's blatant campness something of a release. The grotesquely thin actor was known to have stopped one party dead by enquiring, in his piping voice, 'Anyone fancy a spot of buggery?' Whale also freely admitted that he liked Thesiger because he was related to aristocracy (later in life Thesiger became a great friend of Queen Mary, on whom he modelled his appearance), and Whale loved to associate himself with the genuine article. A gentleman's status could only be improved by having such people in his circle.

By 1920, Whale had moved on to Stratford-on-Avon, where he performed more Shakespeare and began to acquire some knowledge of stage direction. It was here that he was spotted by the famous Nigel Playfair who invited Whale to join another rep company, this time in Liverpool. He began to move between Liverpool and London, acting, designing and eventually becoming Playfair's stage-manager at the Savoy Theatre.

Whale made his debut for Playfair in September 1922 in Arnold Bennett's *Body and Soul*. Playing Lady Mab Infold in the production was Viola Tree ('The tall Tree in sandals') who grabbed the attention of the *Daily Sketch*'s Keble Howard:

> A poseuse and notoriety hunter, who spends half her life being photographed and interviewed for the Press, and goes in for spiritualism and every other craze of the moment. She seems to be quite incorrigible for, in spite of numerous vicissitudes, the end of the play finds her deciding to go to America in order to deliver a series of lectures on herself!

At about this time, Playfair decided to stage *The Insect Play* by the brothers Capek. In the cast was the rising star of English eccentricity, Elsa Lanchester. She was then running a nightclub with Harold Scott in Charlotte Street, London, which they dubbed 'The Cave of Harmony'. Without the benefit of a drinks licence, she remembered how they took to leaving the tops off bottles of cider in the hope that a fortnight's exposure might make them a little alcoholic:

> It was a lovely fire-trap, illuminated only by candlelight. Sometimes we did a midnight one-act play and sometimes we

put together a cabaret show. We had a little trio of violin, piano, and drums, and where the dancing stopped, people sat on the floor to watch the show.[8]

Into this bohemian whirl came many famous people including H G Wells, Aldous Huxley, Evelyn Waugh and, of course, James Whale: '[Whale] was a wonderful tango dancer and he always danced with Zinkeisen'.[9] Whale's mysterious partner was Doris Zinkeisen, scenic designer of *The Insect Play* and his constant companion during those heady days. An extraordinary personality, Zinkeisen was destined to be the only woman in Whale's life.

You can scarcely imagine your surprise when you first meet Doris Zinkeisen and hear her speak. Slinky, exotic-looking, bearer of an exotic name, and deriving her ancestry mainly from French, English, Flemish, and Austrian forebears, she answers you in the faint burr of Dumbartonshire. With light-green eyes, swan-like neck, black hair brushed back, and large, shapely hands, she instantly arrests attention as she enters a room.[10]

Doris Clare Zinkeisen was born at Kilcreggan, Scotland on 31 July 1898. She won a scholarship to the Royal Academy School, and at seventeen had her first picture exhibited at the Academy – a portrait of her sister, Anna. 'Of Flemish extraction, she looks Slav, speaks with a Scottish accent. Very slender, very dark. Sleeps and eats little. Is a connoisseur of old brandy.'[11]

Also in the cast of *The Insect Play* was a young John Gielgud, who recalled the woman to whom Whale was eventually to become engaged:

The rehearsals at the Regent were very exciting. It was thrilling to play a part that had never been played by anyone before, and to see the production taking shape. Claude Rains was in the cast, to my great delight, and also Angela Baddeley, Maire O'Neill, Elsa Lanchester, and Bromley Davenport. Playfair had just discovered at Liverpool Doris Zinkeisen, who was to make her first success in London with her brilliant scenery and dresses for this play. Miss Zinkeisen was very good-looking and wore exotic clothes.[12]

James Whale impressed Gielgud as

> a tall young man with side-whiskers and suede shoes, who was stage-managing for Playfair at the Savoy. ... We met properly at Oxford where he was scenic designer for James B Fagan's Repertory Company and I acted there for three seasons. He played the part of Epihodov in *The Cherry Orchard*, and was then engaged to Doris Zinkeisen, a talented and handsome stage designer. I met them both at Sir Nigel Playfair's house.[13]

The house in question was Thurloe Lodge off the Brompton Road which Zinkeisen decorated for Playfair. Gielgud recalled that Whale and his fiancée made 'a striking pair at the dances to which Playfair, with his charming hospitality, used to invite the company ... '.[14]

James Whale's relationship with Doris Zinkeisen remains one of the great mysteries of his life. Their engagement may have been a mere whim: the familiar close friendship between a gay man and a sympathetic woman friend, or, as happens occasionally, an unusually intense heterosexual interlude in an otherwise homosexual nature. Although they were very much an item in the mid-1920s, it seems unlikely that Whale was attempting to suppress his true nature. He remained engaged to Zinkeisen but, secure in the friendly atmosphere of the theatrical world, began seeking male lovers.

Notes

1. 'Master of Horror', *Black Country Bugle*, April 1981.
2. Elsa Lanchester, *Elsa Lanchester Herself* (London: Michael Joseph, 1983).
3. Peter Barnsley, 'James Whale', *The Black Countryman*, summer 1969.
4. Ibid.
5. Alan Napier, interview with Gregory Mank; quoted in *Frankenstein* script book (New Jersey: Magic Image Film Books, 1989).

9: *Man with Red Hair*

6. William Thomaier, 'James Whale', *Films in Review*, 1962.
7. Ernest Thesiger, Obituary of James Whale, *The Times*, June 1957.
8. Lanchester, *Elsa Lanchester Herself*.
9. Ibid.
10. Charles Gay, 'Celebrities in Cameo – No. 95: Doris Zinkeisen', *The Bystander*, 1935.
11. Obituary of Doris Zinkeisen, *Sunday Telegraph*, 6 January 1991.
12. John Gielgud, *Early Stages* (London: Macmillan, 1939).
13. John Gielgud, letter to the author, 13 October 1993.
14. Gielgud, *Early Stages*.

Chapter two

AS John Gielgud recalled, he first met Whale when the two went to work with the Oxford Players. Whale was there for three seasons, beginning in 1924, under the benevolent eye of James Bernard Fagan ('an Irishman of great personal charm', according to Gielgud, he and Playfair 'understood actors very well'). The 'delightful' company included Tyrone Guthrie, Veronica Turleigh, Flora Robson, Richard Goolden, Reginald Denham, Alan Napier, Glen Byam Shaw, Mary Grey, Dorothy Green, Doris Lytton, Minnie Rayner and Raymond Massey.

Fagan mounted several innovative productions before his untimely death, including work by Wilde, Congreve, Pirandello, Synge and the first successful British staging of Chekhov's *The Cherry Orchard*. Gielgud recalled the working environment:

> We acted on a tiny stage, which Fagan had cleverly built out in an 'apron' several feet in width, with side doors leading on to it. There was no front curtain, except to the inner stage, and any properties needed on the forestage used to be 'set' in view of the audience by a stage hand in a white coat like a cricket umpire ... [1]

There was some talk of Whale becoming assistant director but, in the event, Fagan controlled every production.

> There was no foyer, and smoking was not allowed, so ... that we relied principally on the faithful few who patronized us regularly with season tickets. On the other hand we presented a very interesting programme and the company acted increasingly well together. Reginald Denham and

James Whale helped Fagan with the producing, and Fagan and Whale took turns in designing the scenery, which we all used to help paint and construct between Saturday night and Monday afternoon. Some of the effects were quite ambitious. Whale did a wood for *Deirdre of the Sorrows* consisting almost entirely of a few light tree-trunks cut in three-ply, and we had a most regal tent scene in *Monna Vanna*, contrived from the rose-coloured curtains used by Fagan at the Court Theatre for the Moscovitch *Merchant of Venice* Trial Scene.[2]

The company put on a new play every week, tying in with the academic terms. If the work failed to make it to the West End, or a holiday arrived, the company would split up until called back for a new project.

Whale, in addition to his production and designing chores, played parts in two plays which *did* make it to the West End. *A Comedy of Good and Evil* and *The Cherry Orchard*. The first featured Alan Napier and Whale as a Welsh priest, 'Gas' Jones, who takes in a beautiful young orphan of the storm, played by James Fagan's daughter, Gamma. Later he discovers that she is the child of the Devil and Jones must make a decision between his Christian charity and his true beliefs.

The play was well received but did little business, and the company disbanded again. Alan Napier and the other members of the Oxford Players who had families to go back to often wondered how Whale spent his time during these enforced breaks. Whenever the company came back together, there was the enigmatic Whale, ready to work. On a wage of eight pounds a week, Whale was not well off, and was most likely living in an assortment of dingy bedsits at this time. Indeed the realism and detail which he brought to the seedy interiors of his *Waterloo Bridge* (1931) speak of a very real familiarity with such an existence.

Alan Napier became great friends with Whale and watched with interest as he carefully constructed his persona by adopting the speech patterns and mannerisms of what Napier referred to as Whale's 'gentleman lovers'. Unfortunately, there is scant evidence as to the identity of these elusive men. Were they other actors who, like

Ernest Thesiger, happened to have the necessary aristocratic credentials? Or were they the genuine article, wealthy or titled theatre-goers able to teach Whale about etiquette and good manners? Despite the success of his ongoing transformation from working-class boy to English gentleman, Whale is unlikely to have mixed freely with those born to such an existence. One such man was writer and critic J R Ackerley, in whose *Prisoners of War* Whale was to perform a few years later. The 1920s were roaring loudly and Ackerley, a prosperous middle-class young man, was able to socialize with a number of wealthy homosexuals, including E M Forster, W J H Sprott, Gerald Heard, Christopher Wood, L E O Charlton and Tom Wichelo.

> This group, along with such satellites as Raymond Mortimer, Eddy Sackville-West, Francis Birrell, Lionel Fielden, Duncan Grant and a number of theatre people – John Gielgud, Robert Harris, Robert Helpmann – formed a raffish and intellectual circle that racketed around London, visiting cinemas, theatres, concerts, the zoo and the Ring in Blackfriars Road. ... They had their favourite pubs, notably the York Minster in Soho's Old Compton Street, and their favourite restaurants: The Cafe Royal; the Criterion, which did a good three and sixpenny lunch; the Isola Bella in Greek Street; and Gennaro's in New Compton Street, famous for its beautiful waiters, who were carefully selected by the flamboyant old proprietor during holidays back in his native Italy.[3]

John Gielgud insisted that he knew nothing about Whale's private life, so it seems unlikely that Whale ever became part of such a circle. It is tempting to wonder, however, whether Whale formed his own version of this kind of group, visiting favourite, if somewhat cheaper haunts with his own friends. Although Whale was always discreet, the relaxed and tolerant atmosphere of the theatre may have made a promiscuous gay lifestyle comparatively easy. What is certain is that Whale, by then thirty-five but looking younger, developed a wide circle of gay friends. His lifelong interest was in younger men, and Alan Napier remembered being taken by Whale to a gay party during the run of *A Comedy of Good and Evil* where, he was promised, someone was *very* interested in his broad shoulders. Naive and eager to please, Napier dutifully attended but afterwards decided he was quite definitely heterosexual, much to the chagrin of Whale, who had developed a real liking for his handsome 22-year-old colleague.

In May 1925, James Fagan decided to embark upon Chekhov's *The Cherry Orchard*, which had only ever received one previous disastrous production, during which most of the audience had walked out. It had been produced by the Stage Society, one of several private theatre clubs formed to take advantage of the absence of any professional theatre on the Sabbath. This system, free from censorship, led to bold and innovative performances of works unlikely to find backing elsewhere. Shaw's *Captain Brassbound's Conversion* and *Mrs Warren's Profession* were first produced under this system.

Undeterred by the reception given to the Stage Society's version, Fagan assembled his cast, which included Alan Napier, Mary Grey, James Whale (as Epihodov) and John Gielgud (as Trofimov):

> *The Cherry Orchard* made a stir at Oxford, and Playfair, who came to see it, offered to transfer the whole production to the Lyric, Hammersmith, at the end of the Oxford season. The prospects of success were not very hopeful, however. . . . at the dress rehearsal at Hammersmith the backers smoked many cigarettes and shook their heads over the booking sheets.[4]

After a slow start, however, *The Cherry Orchard* took off tremendously, moving to the Royalty in Dean Street and running throughout the summer. James Agate reviewed it enthusiastically, both in print and in one of his famous wireless addresses; but Basil MacDonald Hastings called it the worst play in London. With characteristic showmanship, Fagan and Playfair displayed the contrasting notices side by side; the public was intrigued and the play ran for 136 performances.

During *The Cherry Orchard*'s run, Whale was asked to perform and design at the Court Theatre in J R Ackerley's *Prisoners of War*, a strange and rather morbid play concerning an officer's unhealthy adoration of a younger man while both are incarcerated in a Swiss camp. After being turned down by the Stage Society, Ackerley's work had finally been picked up by a similar body: Phyllis Whitworth's Three Hundred Club. Although outside his own experience of the conflict, the play must have proven poignant for Whale, as its theme was both radical and unmistakable:

> In December 1924, Ackerley went with [Goldsworthy Lowes] Dickinson to see the opening play in the Three Hundred Club season, and was alarmed to find that it was very poorly produced. Furthermore, Mrs Whitworth's assertion that the play was about jealousy turned out to be something of a misconception; quite clearly the theme was sadism. Ackerley reflected that if the first play was sadistic, the second (W J Turner's *Smaragda's Love*) androgynous, and the third (his own play) homosexual, then Mrs Whitworth was certainly breaking new ground; but he also wondered whether this was an accident rather than design.[5]

Whale played Jellerton in the play, alongside Raymond Massey, Colin Keith-Johnstone, Carleton Hobbs and Robert Harris. John Gielgud attended the first night. Although depicting a very different war to his own in the trenches, the notion of men confined so closely together and the strong attachments formed therein must have struck a chord with Whale. Indeed, the strong, comradely bonding seen in so much of Whale's work, particularly *Journey's End*, may have found its roots in Ackerley's extraordinary play.

Prisoners of War was the talk of London for a while, becoming known as 'the new homosexual play'. Ackerley, meanwhile, was hailed as a 'true disciple of Ibsen'. Stephen Spender recalled how Christopher Isherwood had talked excitedly about it whilst sunbathing on Rügen Island.

The reviews were excellent, and most were able to recognize the principal theme of the play ('the least understood of abnormalities', wrote James Agate). Others, however, were shocked and baffled. The critic St John Ervine wrote:

> A singular friendship which had grown between Conrad and his junior, Grayle, is about to collapse and Conrad, a highly-strung, introspective, worrying man, is upset about it. Mr Ackerley does not attempt to explain how this friendship began; he presents it to us as fact. I found myself refusing to believe in it. Grayle, a lad of 19, is a mean little snipe who does not display a single fine quality in the whole course of the play. ... How a man of fine feeling could make a close friendship of this obnoxious youth is something which I cannot understand.[6]

This particular review must have been read with some amusement: the St John Ervines of the time, of course, never would understand.

Prisoners of War transferred to the Playhouse Theatre, Charing Cross on 1 September 1925, but ran for only twenty-four performances. The theatre-going public, it seemed, was not yet ready for the love which dare not speak its name.

When Whale finally left the Oxford company, he moved into a flat at 402a, King's Road, Chelsea. His friend R C Sherriff recalled the humble accommodation:

> They were modest rooms, very much the quarters of a man who lived for the theatre. Framed around the walls were coloured sketches of stage sets that he had designed for various productions; his bookcase was full of printed plays, his table piled with manuscripts.[7]

Whale was rapidly becoming a jack of all trades: designing sets, costumes and performing, albeit in minor roles. Increasingly, however, his mind was turning towards another ambition: direction. While looking for an opening, he designed sets, costumes and played Medvedenko in *The Sea Gull* at the Little Theatre, followed by the very odd *Mr Godly Beside Himself* for the Three Hundred Club, in which he played Harry Le Poon. This comedy opened on 28 February 1925 to rather baffled notices: 'A comedy without a moral, and, as I did not hear the high-brows laugh ... I presume it must have been a farce.... In green tights and performing queer elocutions, Mr Godley is quite incomprehensible.'

Following this, Whale embarked on *Riverside Nights*, a hugely popular Nigel Playfair revue for which he once again designed sets and costumes. An extremely bizarre mixture of song and dance, drama, opera and satire, the cast included Miles Malleson, Elsa Lanchester and Whale himself, this time playing a parody of Chekhov's *The Three Sisters*. Although the revue received excellent notices – the Chekhov parody receiving particular praise – *The Times* noted, 'Mr James Whale stood oddly out of the picture, as if you had put a real vase into a still life, for his part was almost a reproduction of his Epikhodov [*sic*].'

Whale kept himself busy, designing for the Three Hundred Club's *Don Juan*, performing in Molière's *The Would-Be Gentleman*, adapted from the original *Le Bourgeois Gentilhomme*, and contributed both talents to Nigel Playfair's production of Farquhar's *The Beaux' Stratagem*.

1927 was again a busy, if uninspired year. Whale designed another Three Hundred Club production, this time D H Lawrence's biblical epic *David*, directed by Ernest Milton. Following this, in May, Whale worked with his friend Miles Malleson again, this time as Collins the butler in *Love at Second Sight*, but the play was not a success. He rounded off the year designing and acting in *The Kingdom of God* at the Strand. It must have been terribly galling for Whale, now thirty-eight, to be continually relegated to minor roles. If his future lay in the theatre, then what was he to do? Design obscure private productions? Make rare West End appearances in small roles? Whale must have sensed that directing was the route he must take if he were to make anything of his life.

In 1928, Whale appeared in a number of productions that were seemingly tailor-made for his love of the bizarre and grotesque. The first was a controversial adaptation of Hugh Walpole's *Portrait of a Man with Red Hair*: an extraordinary and almost indefensibly nasty novel concerning a sadist's imprisonment of two lovers in his cliff-top house, and the pain, both physical and mental, which he inflicts upon them. The play was written by Benn Levy and starred

Charles Laughton as the insane Crispin: 'a very gargoyle of obscene desires', according to the *Manchester Guardian*.

In this 'romantic macabre', Whale played Laughton's son (though he was actually ten years the actor's senior), described in the novel as 'thin, white, the nose long pointed, a dark, almost grotesque shadow'. 'Mr James Whale', continued the *Guardian* review, 'and Mr George Bealby, too, are extremely effective. Mr Whale's facial expression is, astonishingly various and impressive'. While the *Sunday Times* noted of Whale that, 'All doting and masochistic compliance were in that restless mask and those twisted hands.'

The play was a considerable, if controversial, success. Whale remembered that a shocked Hugh Walpole came backstage after the first night claiming, 'I ... didn't know what I'd written. I didn't know what I'd written!' 'What nonsense!' said Whale later. 'Of course he knew!'

'Cruelty and torture dominate the stage,' wrote *The Times*. 'There is no escaping from it. Mr Laughton's acting we are bound to admire, but we owe an evening of something very near misery to its skill.' The production was not without its lighter moments, however. Elsa Lanchester remembered Laughton spending hours under the Charing Cross arches practising with a bullwhip which, she confessed, slightly nauseated her. Whale himself, years later, recounted to friends a moment which amused him greatly:

> Jimmy said that Laughton had this frightful scene, I suppose in that period it must've been done with some discretion, but Laughton, in effect, *masturbated* on stage. He was blubbering and slobbering and puffing and Jimmy said, 'And then *I* had to come on. Nobody even noticed me!'[8]

Through his friendship with Elsa Lanchester, Whale got to know Laughton well but, though always cordial, they never really cared for one another. A tortured homosexual, Laughton was filled with self-loathing and found Whale's easy-going acceptance of his own sexuality rather difficult to take. He had seen Whale perform in the Molière play and, aware of his working-class origins, began to refer disparagingly to him as the 'Would-Be Gentleman'.

The second delight for Whale that year was to appear in the only British version of the legendary French Grand Guignol theatre. The splendid, gory tosh which so delighted Parisian audiences right up to the Second World War did not, however, go down too well in London. Whale appeared in three performances of *The Old Firm's Awakening* and twenty-three performances of *After Death*, in which he played a corpse who is brought back to life using electricity. It is no coincidence that Whale should have had a hand in the two most celebrated theatrical grotesques of the day and the influence of such work on his later films cannot be stressed too highly.

Following the Stage Society's worthy *Paul Among the Jews*, Whale was asked to play the title role in *Fortunato*, which Anmer Hall was producing at the Court Theatre in tandem with *The Lady from Alfaqueque*. A tragic farce and a straight comedy, the plays had been translated from Serafin and Joaquin Alvárez Quintero's original Spanish by Harley Granville-Barker and his wife Helen. Unexpectedly, Anmer Hall then asked Whale to direct the plays. This was the chance he had been waiting for.

In the cast were Margaret Webster, Anthony Ireland, Miriam Lewes, Gracie Leigh, Elsie French and, yet again, John Gielgud. Whale threw himself into the task, and the company worked long and hard. Then, unexpectedly, things changed, as John Gielgud recalled:

> we were hard at work when we heard one morning that the Granville-Barkers were coming to a rehearsal. When the day arrived and Barker sat in the stalls, we were all extremely nervous. Everyone whispered, people smoothed their hair and walked about, and Miriam Lewes sat, dressed in her best frock, beating a tattoo with her fingers on the arm of her chair. Barker was certainly a revelation. He rehearsed us for about two hours, changed nearly every move and arrangement of the stage, acted, criticized, advised, in an easy flow of practical efficiency, never stopping for a moment.[9]

It was a devastating experience for first-time director Whale, but worse was to come:

We all sat spellbound, trying to drink in his words of wisdom and at the same time to remember all the hints he was giving us, none of which we had time to write down or memorize. Even when he announced that James could not possibly play Fortunato and that O B Clarence must be engaged, everyone gasped but nobody ventured to disagree.[10]

Humbled by the experience and 'deeply disappointed' according to Gielgud, Whale could do nothing. In the event, though well received, the plays did little business. *The Times* made a point, however, of the decoration and production of Mr James Whale, 'who never fails to make his own manner an accompaniment to the dramatists' melody and an enrichment of it.'

Despite Granville-Barker's interference, Whale's work on the two plays led to another offer to direct, this time Anthony Mervyn's strange play *The Dreamers*. His cast of four were Gwen Ffrangcon-Davies, Clare Harris, Sidney Seaward and Ernest Milton. Although unhampered by the playwright this time, Whale was simultaneously directing the play and appearing in *High Treason* at the Strand. Unable to concentrate adequately on either, *The Dreamers* failed to stir any interest.

While appearing at the Strand, Whale was offered a third directing job, this time by Geoffrey Dearmer of the Stage Society. Designed to be their December production, the play had been turned down by all the big-name directors who usually liked to give a few weeks to the production of a worthy, if uncommercial Stage Society venture. It was a 'measure of their desperation', according to the play's author R C Sherriff,[11] that they should finally offer it to Whale. The play was *Journey's End*, and it was to change his life for ever.

Notes

1. John Gielgud, *Early Stages* (London: Macmillan, 1939).
2. Ibid.
3. Peter Parker, *Ackerley – A Life of J R Ackerley* (London: Constable & Co., 1989).

4. Gielgud, *Early Stages*.
5. Parker, *Ackerley*.
6. St John Ervine, review, 1928, Theatre Museum, Covent Garden.
7. R C Sherriff, *No Leading Lady* (London: Victor Gollancz, 1968).
8. Curtis Harrington, interview with the author, Los Angeles, September 1993.
9. Gielgud, *Early Stages*.
10. Ibid.
11. Sherriff, *No Leading Lady*, p. 62.

Chapter three

James Whale was a very strange personality. He was tall and thin and had a face like a rather nice-looking monkey. (Not a bad-looking monkey!) He was a bitter man – very bitter. I think it was because he had been in love with a lady painter. ... He and Zinkeisen were engaged to be married, but at some point around the time of *Journey's End*, they parted. I don't think James Whale ever got over it ... I think he believed that was to blame for his not having a 'normal' life.[1]

Elsa Lanchester's rather naive interpretation of Whale's decision not to marry Doris Zinkeisen seems rather unlikely. There was no falling out between Whale and Zinkeisen, and they remained great friends following her marriage to Captain Grahame Johnstone DSC in 1927 until the end of Whale's life. Whale needed to be in control. It was the dominant factor in his life, and he was unhappy whenever his independence was threatened. What seems most likely to have occurred is that Whale rejected a marriage which would have been purely for the sake of public appearance, preferring rather to completely accept his homosexuality. Ernest Thesiger, by contrast, did the decent thing and became a very unlikely bridegroom. Elsa Lanchester's assertion that Whale was bitter is not borne out by the testimony of his closest friends. He seemed perfectly at ease with himself and, as Alan Napier attested, was quite capable of some amusingly camp bitchiness concerning the sexuality of his colleagues. What is certain is that about the time he became involved with *Journey's End*, the sharply dressed, satanically good-looking Whale had fallen in love with someone else. This was a young man of around twenty-one years of age named Robert Barthe Offen.

'Bobby' Barthe, as he was known, was an amateur actor whose entire stage experience seems to have been at the famous St Pancras Peoples' Theatre in Tavistock Place, London. Designed as a community theatre, the St Pancras was inaugurated in 1927 by Edith Neville with the bold intention to produce 'a new play every week' for those unable to afford West End prices. 'The Theatre', she wrote, 'is the most potent cultural influence in modern life and no community can afford to let it be neglected or debased'.[2]

Bobby Barthe made his debut at the St Pancras Peoples' Theatre in Bayard Veiller's *Within the Law* on 14 June 1928, and played everything from a sergeant in Shaw's *The Devil's Disciple* (1929) to Toad in *Toad of Toad Hall* (1933). By the late 1930s, he had graduated to the title roles in Molière's *Tartuffe* and Shakespeare's *Henry VIII*. Barthe's last recorded appearances are in Isherwood and Auden's *Ascent of F6* and the final St Pancras pantomime, *Babes in the Wood* in 1939.

It was in the *early* 1930s, however, that an actor called Abbot Chamberlain came to work at the theatre. Later to change his name to John Abbott and destined to meet James Whale years later in Hollywood, he recalled the slender young man who had so infatuated Whale:

> The St Pancras was semi-amateur. Maurice Evans came from there. Michael Hordern and André Morell too. Well, when I joined, I went to see one of their productions and a young fellow named Robert Barthe Offen was playing in it. When I joined the company I got to know the other actors, including Bobby. He was a beautiful, golden-haired boy. And he was always going on about Jimmy Whale, who had been one of his closest friends in the late Twenties. Bobby invited me to his house one day and he had a nice old mum who was a char-lady or something and she was going on about Jimmy this and Jimmy that. Jimmy, Jimmy, Jimmy! Bobby Barthe and James Whale had a very good time together, I'm sure, and Bobby once gave me a vivid description of he and Jimmy

romping about in bed together which I'm afraid wild horses wouldn't drag out of me – even today![3]

Further details on Robert Barthe Offen are few and far between. He never acted professionally and is thought to have got into some sort of financial trouble. His relationship with Whale, who was by then nearly forty, remains the earliest documented liaison, and demonstrates that Whale was continuing his interest in much younger men.

However long the love affair with Bobby Barthe lasted, by 1928 Whale was concentrating on his new directing assignment, *Journey's End*:

> It was ideal for the playwright, but a more unappetising set-up for a commercial manager would have been difficult to find. In those days the theatre worked in colourful, romantic surroundings. The producer staked a lot on the attractive design of his scenes, making them as eye-catching and alluring as possible. A dirty, gloomy dug-out lit with candles; no furniture beyond a rickety wooden table and a few upturned boxes for seats; no love interest; no plot; and no women in the cast; you could scarcely have done better if you had set out deliberately to make the thing as repulsive to a manager as possible.[4]

So recalled the author of *Journey's End*, R C 'Bob' Sherriff, who was working for the Sun Insurance Company when he decided to chronicle some of his experiences in the trenches in the form of a play. He had written seven previous plays, originally to provide funds for the Kingston Rowing Club of which he was a passionate member. After successfully producing these few amateur efforts, Sherriff began to look around for an agent, while ever cautiously, seeking to advance himself at the Sun Insurance office. He was eventually taken on by the agents Curtis Brown, but his work had yet to meet with anything other than polite rejection. Happy enough in his job (as an 'outdoor man', which entailed chasing up late payments and soothing the worries of troubled shareholders), Sherriff's ambitions to write were starting to dwindle, when an idea began to nag away in the back of his mind. He set to work on a novel: his theme, he wrote, 'was hero worship, and the story began with two boys at school. The elder boy, Dennis Stanhope, was the hero; and Jimmy Raleigh worshipped him from afar.'[5]

The original story followed the promising Stanhope's drift into dissolution and the desperate Raleigh's attempts to save his fallen idol. The novel began well enough, but Sherriff soon got cold feet. It just didn't seem to speak truthfully to him. Eventually, he returned to the idea of a play and this time changed the setting to an environment he knew only too well:

> The other characters walked in without invitation. I had known them all so well in the trenches that the play was an open house for them. Raleigh would not have been old enough to arrive at the front before the last year of the war, so the story fell naturally into the most dramatic episode on the Western front: the days before the final, desperate attack on the Germans in March 1918.[6]

Sherriff worked on it for a year until he was absolutely satisfied. He structured the play to take place over three days, chronicling the young Raleigh's arrival at Stanhope's dugout, where he finds his boyhood hero an embittered alcoholic. Stanhope resents this link to his past, especially as he is devoted to Raleigh's sister. The play ends with both their deaths: Raleigh, expiring in his hero's arms, and Stanhope himself, crushed by the roof of the dugout after a shell detonates above it. It was a sombre, wilfully uncommercial play, but to Sherriff it spoke truthfully of the horrors of war, of the men he had fought alongside and his own very personal memories of them.

After consulting a couple of friends, neither of whom thought it had any potential as a play, he cautiously sent it to Curtis Brown. To his astonishment they wrote back saying it was 'very fine' and 'we shall do everything possible to secure its performance'. Sherriff was elated, but there was a major obstacle looming. No play about the war had ever been a commercial success. The public, it was felt, did not want to be reminded of such horrors. *Journey's End*, which broke all the rules of established theatre, seemed a particularly unlikely property.

After approaching several leading actors for the role of Stanhope, without success, Curtis Brown sent the play to the Stage Society, and this time something came of it. Sherriff went along to see the Stage Society's *Paul Amongst the Jews*, which featured James Whale in the cast. At this stage, however, Sherriff was more interested in meeting Geoffrey Dearmer, a member of the Society committee. In the interval, Dearmer told him he thought *Journey's End* a 'wonderful play and it'll be a sheer tragedy if it isn't produced'.

Unfortunately, the committee were well aware of the received wisdom on war plays, and weren't too keen to proceed. Dearmer recommended that Sherriff send the play to George Bernard Shaw as his opinion might lend weight to their argument. Without much hope, the nervous author followed his advice, and, uncharacteristically, Shaw sent back both Sherriff's stamps and a detailed critique. He considered the play more of a historical document than a work of art, but nevertheless ended his comments with 'let it be produced by all means'.

Delighted that the great man had taken time to consider his humble effort, Sherriff reported back to Geoffrey Dearmer. But Shaw's qualified recommendation wasn't, in the end, necessary. The committee had had a change of heart and wanted to produce *Journey's End*.

The offer to James Whale to direct the play was no flattering proposal based on Whale's previous successes. The reality was that no one else would touch it. The Stage Society had little to lose. The play was determinedly uncommercial, so why not give it to a fledgling director like Whale?

Sherriff was told to go and see Whale at the Strand, and the two first met in Whale's dressing-room where he was making up for his part in *High Treason*:

> He scarcely looked at me; he kept his eyes on the mirror as he rubbed on the grease paint, and talked to my reflection in the glass where I sat in a chair behind him. He didn't seem very enthusiastic about *Journey's End*. I gathered that it was a

stop-gap production because the one originally planned by the Stage Society for December was a big expensive affair postponed for a month to get the right people to act in it. He was also no doubt aware that *Journey's End* had been turned down by all the established directors, and that he too was a stop-gap for the want of anybody else.[7]

Whale's coolness about *Journey's End* was characteristic. He was never one to gush, but he did, in fact, greatly admire the play and was very excited at the prospect of working on something so close to his own experience. He informed Sherriff that some parts were 'too sentimental' and would have to be changed or excised entirely. Sherriff readily agreed. He would, he said, have rewritten the whole thing if it had any prospect of getting closer to the West End:

> He began to thaw out when he found out that I wasn't going to argue about the things he wanted to do. He told me that he had been an infantry officer and served in the actual line of trenches where the play was set. He didn't say he liked the play, but I soon found out he had read it very thoroughly and already knew it backwards.[8]

The next day, Sherriff called round to Whale's flat in the King's Road to see the 'beautifully constructed model' which Whale had built for the set design:

> I had envisaged little more than a squalid cavern in the ground, but Whale had turned the hand of art to it. By strutting the roof with heavy timbers he gave an impression of vast weight above: an oppressive, claustrophobic atmosphere with a terrifying sense of imprisonment for those who lived in it. Yet with this, through innumerable small details, he had given it a touch of crude romance that was fascinating and exhilarating. Above all it was real. There may never have been a dugout like this one: but any man who lived in the trenches would say: 'This is it: this is what it was like'.[9]

Sherriff felt sure that a more established director would never have bothered with such detail, but Whale, eager to prove his diligence *and* as a veteran of the trenches was, by pure serendipity, the perfect director for *Journey's End*.

With the production under way, Whale turned to the problem of casting. As with the directors, all the established names approached by the Stage Society had turned the play down. As Sherriff recalled, Whale was given a free hand to choose his actors, and, aware that the play had been written off as a stop-gap, he felt able to experiment:

> from Whale's point of view it was exactly what he wanted. He was convinced that the key-note of the play was realism, and he couldn't get that if the characters were overshadowed by the names of the actors playing them. He wanted the audience to see a group of soldiers in a dugout rather than an assembly of well-known actors playing the parts of soldiers, and he set out to cast the play regardless of established reputations. He went for actors free from theatrical tricks and produced for the Stage Society a hand of trumps.[10]

These 'trumps' included George Zucco, St Pancras's Maurice Evans and, in the principal role of the alcoholic Captain Stanhope, the 21-year-old Laurence Olivier.

The then unknown Olivier was playing in John Drinkwater's *Bird in Hand* at the Royalty and leaped at the chance of such a considerable role, though he didn't think much of the play. 'There's nothing in it but meals!' he complained to Whale. 'That's what it was like!' retorted the director. Olivier's only condition was that Whale should persuade the distinguished director Basil Dean to attend the performance. Despite his reservations about the play, he obviously recognized that a part like Stanhope offered a rare chance to impress Dean.

Whale called the first read-through in a room above a shop in Charing Cross Road. Bob Sherriff, who had little experience of professional theatre and actors, was rather dismayed by the sight of the shabby room and the assembled cast. Whale sat at a bare table in an overcoat and muffler, the cast, an 'ordinary looking lot of men;

what you might see any evening waiting at Waterloo Station for a train home', mingled around him. Olivier was huddled over the tiny fire, struggling to keep warm and looking, Sherriff thought, as though he wished he hadn't turned up.

Before the reading began, the actor engaged to play Mason, the cook-batman, strolled in, tossed his script on the table and announced that he had been offered a West End show. It was a perennial problem of the Stage Society shows, and one still encountered by fringe theatre today. Paid work usually takes precedence over unprofitable drama, no matter how worthy. A small fee could be offered for *Journey's End* but it meant a lot of rehearsal for only two performances. Whale shrugged off the disappointment and told his assistant to phone Alexander Field whom he thought a good replacement.

Whale had advised Sherriff to bring a notebook with him – a golden rule for authors at rehearsals – and to tell him if there was anything with which he disagreed. After that first read-through, however, Sherriff was in no doubt. Despite their appearances, huddled round the table in that chilly room, some in mufflers and hats, totally unlike the weary soldiers he had envisaged, the play came alive:

> They sat with their eyes glued to their scripts, puffing cigarettes, never making an attempt to emphasise or dramatise their lines; but as the reading went on it came over beyond any doubt that the team had been perfectly chosen. None had any need to act the parts; they *were* the men; they merely had to be themselves. And luckily no famous star was there to overwhelm the others.[11]

Obviously delighted, Sherriff and Whale went back to Whale's flat to finish the final cuts, which turned out to be very minor indeed. Whale told Sherriff that there was no need for him to come to any more rehearsals unless they ran into problems, in which case he would telephone. In any event, Sherriff had to return to the office, and so the bulk of the work fell on Whale's shoulders.

With a scant two weeks until the performance, and unable to use the stage of the Apollo (where the play would be performed) as the current piece was still in residence, the company began work in rehearsal rooms with the dugout set marked out in chalk. At the end of the fortnight, the crew had to work round the clock to clear the stage and erect the dugout set in time for the Sunday night performance. The actors had seen Whale's model of the set, but there was a serious risk that they would be thrown by the unfamiliar environment and the complicated sound effects which Whale had devised to simulate the noise of shells, bullets and flares.

Sherriff, meanwhile, remained content in his insurance job, confessing that to get a play on in the West End, in however humble circumstance, was beyond his wildest expectations: 'I would have given them everything I'd got; I would have sold my bicycle and sculling boat if they'd needed a bit of extra money'.[12] The Stage Society could have done with his help. The actors were paid £5 each, Whale £10 and the sets cost £80. The theatre came virtually free but the staff had, obviously, to be paid. One advantage of the cast's generation was that genuine uniforms could easily be borrowed. Sherriff lent his own uniform to Olivier. He had been a captain, like Stanhope, though the Military Cross ribbon had to be stitched onto his tunic for the play.

At last, on 10 December 1928, just over ten years since the end of the Great War, *Journey's End* was ready. There was one last frenzied dress-rehearsal, and then the audience began to file in. Sherriff, bathed in nervous sweat under his uncomfortable evening dress, had been given a box with his mother. Unable to bear the tension, he roamed around during the performance, finding himself in the corridor behind the orchestra pit. On his nervous meanderings, he bumped into Whale who seemed as edgy as the author:

> I'd whisper to him, 'How d'you think it's going?', and he'd nod and walk away. He wanted to be alone. His work was done, and nothing remained but to watch and hope. I knew every moment in the play where things were tricky, and easy to go wrong.[13]

Eventually, unable to bear the suspense any longer, and convinced that the dugout steps would collapse under the combined weight of the sergeant-major with the mortally wounded Raleigh in his arms, Sherriff fled into the icy street, pacing up and down until he knew the play was over. His timing was slightly off and the audience were already clapping as he hurried back inside.

The response seemed restrained, polite even, and Sherriff was convinced the audience were anxious to get home. Everything seemed to have gone well: if the applause had been muted then only the play was to blame. Sherriff couldn't bear to talk to Whale or the cast and hurried home, somewhat depressed. His ever-loyal mother praised the play unreservedly and, even allowing for her partiality, Sherriff began to cheer up. Women in the stalls had been crying, she assured him, their white handkerchiefs had shown up in the dark. And people didn't clap when they were crying.

The next day, feeling isolated and nervous, Sherriff phoned Whale:

> He was in a hurry and didn't want to talk. He was just off to the theatre to rehearse some of the sound effects and stage lighting which hadn't satisfied him on the previous night. I asked him how he thought the play had gone and he was non-committal, inclined to brush me off.[14]

Whale was as phlegmatic as ever and assumed a front of indifference, knowing full well the dangers of overconfidence. He told Sherriff that the performance had been beyond his expectations and that everyone concerned had risen to the task. The problem lay with the Stage Society audience, who were undemonstrative and difficult to please. Everyone seemed to have liked and admired the play, including Barry Jackson, but thought it 'too sad and depressing for the public taste'.

Following his morning's work, Sherriff went off to the Monday afternoon performance, but came away even more depressed. The play was beautifully performed, but the theatre was half empty and the audience, though attentive, seemed uninspired. He was convinced that a slice of reality like *Journey's End* was of no interest to the theatre-going public.

After the performance, Sherriff went backstage to thank the

actors and collect his uniform from Olivier. All concerned seemed to have genuinely enjoyed the challenge, but there was a definite air of finality. What chance did this little Sunday Society play have of going on to greater things? Their work over, Sherriff and Whale could only await the critical reaction, which wouldn't appear until the next day's papers came out.

How Whale spent that anxious night we don't know, but Sherriff vividly chronicled his sleepless, haunted hours waiting for the paper-boy to arrive. He took the *Daily Express* and the *Daily Telegraph*, which between them featured the talents of two of the most respected and feared critics of the day: Hannen Swaffer and W A Darlington. Opening the *Express*, Sherriff could find no reference to the production and was, for a moment, slightly relieved that the infamously vitriolic Swaffer hadn't even bothered to come to the play. But then, on looking again, he saw a headline so extraordinary that at first he couldn't believe it: 'THE GREATEST OF ALL WAR PLAYS':

> A new dramatist, R C Sherriff, achieved the distinction of compelling to real emotion an audience who were watching a play almost without a plot, with no women in the cast! ...
> It was a remarkable achievement ... *Journey's End* is perhaps the greatest of all war plays. ... This is the English theatre at its best. ... There is no shirking the facts: no concession to fashion ... it is perfectly acted: each actor cuts a little cameo of stark reality. ... All London should flock to see it. It carries a great lesson – one that is nobly told.

The usually restrained W A Darlington was equally fulsome in his praise; indeed, all the papers who had sent along their critics hailed the play as magnificent. Breathless with excitement, Sherriff phoned Whale, who was just as delighted but rather guarded. Surely something was bound to happen now? 'I don't know,' said Whale, 'but let's hope so.'

The two men had tea together that afternoon in Whale's flat, the model of the dugout set facing them on Whale's sideboard. He told Sherriff that, despite the congratulatory calls he had received from friends, he had heard nothing from any management. He suspected that managers tended to treat fulsome reviews of private plays with caution, as they were aware that critics were sometimes excessive in their praise when a play seemed worthy. It might even have been better if the critics had condemned *Journey's End* because then it would, perforce, seem lowbrow and liable to attract an audience!

It was with mixed emotions, then, that Sherriff listened to James Agate's popular wireless address. To his astonishment, the legendary critic gave over his entire talk to *Journey's End*. It transpired that George Bishop of the *Daily Telegraph* had been to the Monday afternoon performance and, during the interval, had encountered Agate outside, obviously in two minds whether or not to come. 'What's the play like?' he asked Bishop. 'You've got to come in,' said Bishop. 'You've got to see it.' Agate saw the play, returned to his office, tore up his prepared speech and gave *Journey's End* the most unqualified rave he had ever delivered.

Whale listened in rapt disbelief as Agate described how he had never been so deeply moved, so enthralled, so exalted. Poor Sherriff, at home with a dodgy crystal set, struggled to hear through clouds of static. There was no mistaking the tone, though, of what Agate called 'this fine piece of work'. Sherriff rang Whale, who filled in the gaps for him. 'It was tremendous,' said Whale. 'I've never heard Agate talk like that before. If it doesn't do the trick, then nothing will.' But Agate's review had ended with a sad warning, 'you will never see this play. I have spoken with several managers, urging them to give you the opportunity of judging it for yourselves, but they are adamant in their belief that war plays have no audience in the theatre.' Despite this attempt to shame the managers into action, the only positive development threatened, ironically, to spell disaster for any future performances: on the strength of his appearances as Stanhope, Basil Dean offered Olivier the lead in *Beau Geste* and spirited him away.

Whale and Sherriff were despondent. It was almost as though they were cursed with bad luck. How could something so well received simply curl up and die? Agate was convinced that a fortune was awaiting the manager brave enough to produce *Journey's End*, but none seemed willing to take up the gauntlet.

33: *Man with Red Hair*

Days passed and the chances of success dwindled. Curtis Brown tried every manager in town, and the actors even formed a syndicate in the hope of raising the cash to hire a theatre. They were willing to work for nothing until the play paid its way. Then, the day before Christmas Eve, Sherriff received a call from his agents saying that a man named Maurice Browne had called into their offices requesting a copy of the play. Sherriff wasn't initially very enthusiastic about the newcomer's interest. Browne was an unusual man, dedicated to the advancement of poetry and classical drama, who had spent years in America producing worthy, highbrow pieces of little interest to the public. He had returned to England virtually penniless, but had come to the attention of Leonard and Dorothy Elmhirst, patrons of the arts, who had recently established Dartington Hall near Totnes as a kind of proto-arts centre. They liked and admired Browne for his selfless devotion to art for art's sake, and had promised to provide the funds to produce any play he found which popular wisdom decreed unstageable. *Journey's End* wasn't quite the play Browne imagined championing, but everything about its troubled beginnings, wrote Sherriff, 'tied up with his natural instinct to fight for drama with his back to the wall ... for the first time in his life he was free to produce a play without having to pawn his watch and go without his supper'.[15]

Sherriff decided he had nothing to lose and took his only clean copy of the play to Maurice Browne's house in Earl's Court. It was a shabby, unfamiliar area and Sherriff, already uncomfortable from the recently lanced boil on his buttock, began to lose heart. Even if he found the place, how could anyone living in such circumstances be the right man to produce his great work? Eventually, struggling through the bitter cold, Sherriff delivered the play to a suspicious old woman in a downstairs flat.

The next morning saw Sherriff less depressed, and he returned from work feeling quite festive. On the hallstand was a telegram from Maurice Browne:

> *Journey's End* magnificent. Will gladly produce it. Returning to London Monday afternoon. Shall look forward to meeting you without delay. My profound congratulations upon a splendid play.

Sherriff was dumbfounded by this exuberant reaction, and when they met after Christmas, the play's new producer confounded all his expectations. Instead of the seedy aesthete Sherriff had imagined, Browne was an ebullient figure in an expensive coat, gold earrings and an Old Wykehamist tie. 'It's a beautiful play,' Browne told Sherriff. 'Magnificent.'

Suddenly, everything was moving again. Browne advanced Sherriff two hundred pounds for the performance rights and booked the Savoy Theatre in the Strand, where the long run of *Young Woodley* was about to end. Sherriff remained baffled by exactly what it was in *Journey's End* that appealed to Browne. It was completely at odds both with everything he had produced before and his own sentiments regarding war. Browne had been a conscientious objector during the entire conflict and should have objected to the simplistic principle of duty which the characters in the play exemplified:

> Possibly he saw in the play a triumphant justification of his own convictions: that the tragedy and misery of it all would never have happened if every man had stood apart, as he had done, and refused to have anything to do with it.[16]

Browne agreed to take on both the entire original cast (after initially hoping to play Lieutenant Osborne himself) and, of course, James Whale as director. After so long in the sidelines, Whale must have been ecstatic at the chance to direct in the West End.

There was still the problem of replacing Olivier (he was later to cite the role of Stanhope as his favourite), and Whale and Sherriff were worried that the chemistry of the original production might now be lost, especially if a big-name actor were thrust upon them. The two men spent an evening in Whale's flat looking through *Spotlight*, but none of the actors seemed right. Several whom Sherriff liked the look of were known to Whale personally and he dismissed them.

Another dead end loomed, until one evening Maurice Browne received a call from the actress Jeanne de Casalis. Would Whale and Browne care to look at an actor called Colin Clive? The handsome 28-year-old actor was unknown to everyone. In addition, he was engaged to marry de Casalis and the smell of nepotism made everyone wary. Nevertheless, he was asked to read for the part. When he did, Whale and Sherriff knew at once that Clive was their man. His stumbling, halting delivery and edgy, nervous personality endeared him to both men. Despite his bad rendition of the lines, Whale and Sherriff were convinced that Clive must play Stanhope. Maurice Browne thought otherwise. He wanted Colin Keith-Johnstone, who was young, handsome, experienced (he had acted with Whale in Ackerley's *Prisoners of War*) and had won the Military Cross during the actual conflict. To Browne, he appeared tailor-made for the part of Stanhope.

A second reading only served to highlight Clive's short-comings: shuffling his feet, smoking and stumbling over his words, Clive was even worse than before. In contrast, Keith-Johnstone read beautifully in his 'fine, expressive voice'. It appeared that there was no contest:

> Maurice Browne and his manager had no doubts. Whale was thoughtful: something was worrying him, but he didn't know what it was. Maurice Evans, who was to play Raleigh as he had done for the Stage Society, happened to be there and had heard both readings. His part was tied so closely to Stanhope, he had so many vital scenes with him, that his opinion was even more important than ours. He was asked which actor he thought most suited the part. He didn't answer at once. Then he said: 'Keith-Johnstone's got it here' (pointing to his fore-head) – 'but Clive's got it here' (pointing to his heart). [17]

Emboldened by Evans's comments, Whale gave the part to Clive. But it took a long time for the man who was to become Whale's friend and favourite actor, to settle into the role. The nervous qualities which seemed so right for Stanhope were exaggerated in Clive the man. Rehearsals went badly as Clive tried to catch up with the rest of the cast who were, of course, far more familiar with the play. After one particularly bad run, he went to Whale and offered to resign. Convinced that he had made the right choice in casting Clive, Whale would have none of it. But as the days went by and Clive got no better, the entire company were seriously worried. Stanhope was the centre of the play. If he fell, they all fell with him.

Desperate, Sherriff suggested that Clive break his professional code and have a nip of whisky to loosen himself up. It was fine for him to be as highly strung as his character, but if he was too uptight to perform, then there was precious little point in carrying on. Clive was worried, but agreed to give it a try. Over lunch he consumed several whiskies and returned to rehearsals transformed. Lacking only the confidence to command the company, Clive found he was perfectly in tune with his part, uninhibited by nervousness:

> Whale was astonished and delighted: he had always known what a fine performance lay in Clive's power if only it could be released. Now Clive had found himself. He didn't need the whisky for subsequent rehearsals. His performance gained in stature with every day that passed, and Maurice Browne, who had resigned himself to the unhappy conviction that he had put his money on a loser, doubled the money set aside for advertising.[18]

It is interesting to speculate whether this was the beginning of Clive's chronic drink problem. Although, once free of his inhibitions, he no longer needed the whisky for rehearsals of *Journey's End*, it is more than feasible that he became increasingly reliant on drink to shore up his insecurities.

Emboldened, the company moved to the Savoy Theatre, where they had a very bad dress rehearsal, caused principally by the new venue's acoustics playing havoc with Whale's carefully devised sound effects. Sherriff began to panic, convinced that only a last-minute postponement could save the day. Again, Whale remained cool. Despite the shortage of time, he took command of the situation and worked his team incredibly hard to achieve the desired effects. The crew began work at dawn the next morning and only ironed out the last of the problems as the audience were filing in.

When Sherriff arrived at the theatre that night he was expecting chaos. The news that Colin Clive had been knocked down by a bus in the Strand did nothing to calm his nerves. But Clive was fine and already in his dressing-room making up. There were good-luck telegrams from Whale, Browne, the staff of the Sun Insurance Company and, perhaps most poignantly for Sherriff, the members of his beloved rowing club.

In the wings he found Whale, immaculate in evening dress and white carnation buttonhole. 'We did a lot of work this morning,' said Whale, 'and I think everything's all right now.' Whale asked Sherriff to look in on the cast, as they would appreciate a little nod from the author, but to leave Clive alone. Sherriff wandered backstage, where he found an atmosphere of repressed hysteria uncannily reminiscent of the real trenches he had known so well. Finally, it was time for curtain up:

> We opened that night under a friendly star. The threads of luck held good, and Clive's performance was magnificent: more rugged and restrained than Olivier's, but deeply moving, for the actor, like Stanhope himself, was straining every nerve to the utmost limits of endurance to fulfil his task.[19]

In a paroxysm of anxiety, Sherriff spent the last act alternately watching and praying; Whale, in contrast, remained calm in his chosen place next to the stage-manager. As the final curtain came, there was such an overpowering silence that Sherriff confessed he feared the entire audience might be asleep. When a solitary call of 'Bravo' sounded from the auditorium, however, the house went wild. Critics cheered. Even the dreaded 'gallery first-nighters', who more often went to the theatre deliberately to heckle, were moved to cheer. The leading actors, Maurice Evans, George Zucco and, particularly, Colin Clive received tremendous ovations. Whale and Sherriff both made little speeches and then slipped away, the jubilant Whale to the manager's office for celebratory drinks, Sherriff, characteristically, to catch the last train home to his mother.

The reviews the next day were unanimous in their praise. Sherriff fretted again when the flood of ticket-buyers he had expected failed to materialize. He was assured, however, that such things took time, and, by two o'clock that afternoon, business was good and building. The only real worry was the position of the ticket agencies who controlled block bookings and, effectively, the fate of the play. Sherriff was unaware of the complicated behind-the-scenes wrangling already under way when he went to the theatre for the second night:

> Outside in the passage I met James Whale. It wouldn't be a full house that night, he said. The pit and the gallery were full, but most of the booking for the stalls and dress circle was for performances later in the week, mainly for the Saturday night. Had the ticket agencies made a deal, I asked him? 'They've been with Maurice all afternoon,' said Whale, 'and he's turned them down'.
>
> I was incredulous, appalled ... 'Why on Earth?'
>
> Whale shrugged his shoulders. 'I don't know,' he said. 'I don't know why; but I only hope he knows what he's doing.'[20]

In fact, Maurice Browne was taking an incredible gamble. He insisted upon a twelve-week deal which obliged the agencies to buy up so many tickets that a run of the play would be assured. To the old hands in the business, such terms were outrageous. The bookings could dry up at any time, and there was no guarantee that a great critical hit would necessarily transform into a great popular one. *Journey's End* still hadn't disproven the notion that war plays were not liked. The agencies held out in the hope that Browne would crack but, despite warnings from all sides, he stood firm. They balked, breaking off negotiations.

Whale and Sherriff waited anxiously. Then, against all the odds, the die-hard ticket agencies changed their minds and came, cap in hand, to Maurice Browne. The deal he struck was the largest ever for a straight play in the West End, guaranteeing ticket sales of a thousand pounds a week for three months. Every ticket was sold. The play did extraordinary business. Soon, calls were coming in from all over Europe. The Savoy Theatre was packed night after night:

The 'Standing Room Only' boards were brought out half-an-hour before the curtain went up, and 'House Full' went up all round the theatre. The commissionaires enjoyed the excitement of organising the crowds. Nothing like it had happened at the theatre for years. 'When we got out the "House Full" boards for the first time', one said to me, 'we found a mouse's nest behind them.'[21]

All this was incredible for Whale, who must have resigned himself to a fairly inauspicious career prior to the play's success. Suddenly transformed from minor-league actor and stage designer, he was now asked to take *Journey's End* to Broadway.

Notes

1. Elsa Lanchester, interview with Gregory Mank, Los Angeles, 1979; quoted in *Bride of Frankenstein* script book (New Jersey: Magic Image Film Books, 1989).
2. St Pancras Peoples' Theatre brochure, Theatre Museum, Covent Garden.
3. John Abbott, interview with the author, Los Angeles, September 1993.
4. R C Sherriff, *No Leading Lady* (London: Victor Gollancz, 1968), p. 36.
5. Ibid., p. 33.
6. Ibid., p. 35.
7. Ibid., p. 47.
8. Ibid.
9. Ibid.
10. Ibid., p. 49.
11. Ibid., p. 50.
12. Ibid., p. 53.
13. Ibid., p. 54.
14. Ibid., p. 56.
15. Ibid., p. 72.
16. Ibid., p. 73.
17. Ibid., p. 75.
18. Ibid., p. 78.
19. Ibid., p. 84.
20. Ibid., p. 97.
21. Ibid., p. 101.

Chapter four

THE decision to take *Journey's End* across the Atlantic was something of a gamble. It might well have proven too British for American taste, and there was still a lingering resentment over Britain's war debt. American producers, however, had noticed the incredible business the play was doing, and Maurice Browne pulled off yet another coup. The rights went to Gilbert Miller, the only American he felt he could trust to transfer the property unadulterated.

Miller was enthusiastic and diligent. The play would be recast, given a week's try-out in London and then move to New York. The new cast included Jack Hawkins, Leon Quartermaine and, in a very nice gesture, Colin Keith-Johnstone who finally got to play Stanhope. James Whale set about rehearsing his new team and this time everything went smoothly. They spent a week at the Arts Theatre and then boarded the *Aquitania* for America. Sherriff, who had finally given up his job at the Sun Insurance office, went too, Miller insisting that the romance of a clerk writing a West End triumph would be irresistible to the press, and so it proved.

During the crossing, Whale rehearsed in his cabin with small groups of the cast. Most of the time was spent making their accents somewhat more palatable to the new audience. Gilbert Miller warned that if the cast were one hundred per cent English it would be fine. If they were a hundred and five per cent then they would go down the drain.

The cast worked hard as time was very short. As soon as they berthed, there was to be a dress rehearsal at the Henry Miller Theatre. The next day there would be an out-of-town try-out at the Great Neck Playhouse, Long Island, followed on the third day by the Broadway opening. By now, the movement of the dugout set, the operation of the sound effects and the unit of well-rehearsed actors worked steadily and efficiently. So much so that by the time they arrived in Great Neck, a prosperous town on the north shore, there was little left to do but stroll around the beautiful countryside, as Sherriff recalled:

> Even James Whale was at a loose end, no longer needed. Half an hour before the curtain went up he had handed the play over to the stage-manager, as the captain of a ship hands over to a pilot as they come near port. When I got back to the theatre I found him standing outside, hands in pockets, smoking a cigarette. Nothing to do but wait.[1]

It was a tough and nervous performance, a contingent of local boys whistling derisively at young Raleigh's boyish Englishisms. Everyone was worried. If the play were laughed off it would be disastrous for the Broadway premiere. However, the audience settled down once Colin Keith-Johnstone's authoritative Stanhope took the stage, and, by the end, gave *Journey's End* a 'polite and formal' reception. Sherriff felt they had got through, but only by the skin of their teeth.

Back in New York, Sherriff went to visit the American offices of Curtis Brown and then spent the day sitting in Central Park, eyed suspiciously by a passing policeman. When he returned to the rooms he was sharing with Whale, it was obvious that the director was feeling the pressure:

> He was pale and tired, feeling the strain of what amounted to two first nights in succession. Whale was a perfectionist. He would spend time on small details that most people would have thought too trivial to worry about. He had difficulty in getting some of his directions clear to the American stage-hands and technicians. They were friendly and co-operative and knew their jobs, but in some ways they didn't talk the same language, and Whale had to use the stage-manager as an interpreter. It made the work more tiring, but on the whole things had gone well. Everything that could be done had now been done.

We rang down for some sandwiches and a jug of coffee. 'I'd give anything for a whisky and soda', said Whale. But those were the prohibition days, and we hadn't been there long enough to know what steps you took to get a drink.[2]

Nervously, Whale and Sherriff drove to the theatre to take their places for the Broadway premiere. As it turned out, their fears were groundless. The next morning they sat about in their dressing-gowns, devouring the reviews as their ham and eggs grew cold around them. The 'Butchers of Broadway' were unanimous in their praise: 'The finest play to reach Broadway in years' ... 'The best ambassador ever sent to America by Britain.' The phone didn't stop ringing.

The success of *Journey's End* grew apace throughout the summer and autumn of 1929, with fourteen companies playing it in English and seventeen in various European translations, all with tremendous success. A Japanese professor of English was translating the play for Tokyo and the Crown Prince of Siam was doing the same task for Bangkok audiences. Meanwhile, in Holland, the part of Raleigh was played by a girl!

While Sherriff returned home to his mother and a lucrative round of public engagements (turning down, incidentally, an invitation to write the screenplay for *All Quiet on the Western Front*), James Whale was snapped up by Paramount Pictures in New York.

This was a time of no little paranoia in the fledgling film industry, as the coming of sound had created innumerable problems. Hollywood was overflowing with beloved silent stars who simply couldn't cope with dialogue, and directors whose style was no longer suitable for the talking screen. Charles Chaplin seemed particularly worried, as he told *Motion Picture* magazine in March 1929:

Talkies are ruining the oldest art in the world – the art of pantomime. They are ruining the great beauty of silence. They are defeating the meaning of the screen, the appeal that has created the star system, the fan system, the vast popularity of the whole – the appeal of beauty. It's beauty that matters in pictures – nothing else. The screen is pictorial. Pictures. Lovely looking girls, handsome young men in adequate scenes. What if the girls can't act? Of course they can't. They never have. But what of it? Who has cared? Who has known the difference? Certainly I prefer to see, say, Delores Costello [then Mrs John Barrymore] in a thin tale than some aged actress of the stage doing dialogue with revolting close-ups.[3]

Al Jolson, who had started the whole sound revolution with *The Jazz Singer* (1927), responded with a description of a party he had attended in which Chaplin hadn't stopped talking and singing from half-past eight in the evening to five the following morning: 'If he wants to keep what he calls "the great beauty of silence" let him go lock himself in a room, become a nun's brother or something.'

The British, who had thus far struggled against their American counterparts, suddenly found themselves much in demand because of their clear, often stage-trained speaking voices. It was in an effort to give their pictures kudos, also, that the film industry turned to the theatrical world to find new talent. Thus James Whale, the now-famous director of the international hit *Journey's End*, was shunted west to Hollywood. At the fantastic salary of $500 a week, Whale was required to bring his years of experience on the British stage to the upstart medium of film. For Whale, this was a totally unexpected development. To have progressed from directing a two-performance Stage Society piece to a lucrative Hollywood contract in the space of a year would have set anyone's head reeling. Whale was, as ever, restrained. He remembered too well the years of poverty in Dudley and his more recent hand-to-mouth existence in the theatre to suddenly go mad with his new-found wealth.

He was quickly assigned to a silly Richard Dix farce called *The Love Doctor* under the direction of Melville Brown. Whale's task was simply to rehearse the actors' dialogue with them prior to shooting and give them the benefit of his theatrical skills. It must have been a strange time for all concerned as no one had vast experience of the new medium.

Whale was billed as 'dialogue director', and he worked steadily on the picture, learning quickly. He was anxious to gain confidence in film technique so that he would be fully prepared for the direction of the screen version of *Journey's End*, which was being readied for production towards the end of the year. The play's phenomenal success had ensured that the film rights would not go cheaply, but few expected the then record price of £16,000. R C Sherriff let his share of them go for only £2,000, after a protracted and rather nasty argument with Maurice Browne over a verbal agreement the two had made some time before. The rights were sold jointly to Michael Balcon (of Gainsborough Pictures) and Tommy Welsh and George Pearson, who somehow managed to get the money together and beat off the stiff opposition from more established producers. Balcon recalled the venture:

> There was one big snag, however. Welsh-Pearson had no studio, and therefore no means of making a sound film; we had a studio that was not equipped for sound. Both Welsh-Pearson and ourselves were desperately anxious for a success after the financial bashing received by our most recent silent films. It was absolutely imperative for both of us to make the break into the new medium without delay.[4]

Indeed, so primitive were conditions in the fledgling British film industry that a leader in the *Evening Standard* opined: 'Nothing has been done yet in British studios to inspire the belief that work done there could readily be sold to America.'

Thus it was decided that the terribly British *Journey's End* would have to be made in America, and Balcon brokered a contract with the poverty-row studio Tiffany-Stahl. It proved to be a good deal, guaranteeing complete creative control and American theatre bookings of £50,000. A Gainsborough writer–director, V Gareth Gundrey, was assigned to prepare a screenplay, and James Whale was, of course, chosen to direct.

While preparations were proceeding, Paramount again employed Whale as dialogue director, this time on J M Barrie's *The Old Lady Shows Her Medals*. Almost immediately, however, Whale was taken off the picture and loaned out, at considerable profit, to millionaire producer Howard Hughes, who was having a few problems with his ludicrously extravagant Great War flying picture *Hell's Angels*. This extraordinary endeavour, starring Ben Lyon, James Hall and Greta Nissen, had been in production since the autumn of 1927, utilizing 87 planes, 137 pilots, 1700 extras, 35 cameramen and 12 cutters. The script was tailored around the genuinely spectacular flying sequences, but the resulting mess was virtually unwatchable. Hughes decided that something drastic would have to be done if he were to salvage the two million dollars he had ploughed into the project. Most importantly, the coming of sound threatened to make *Hell's Angels* immediately obsolete.

Retaining the aerial sequences, Hughes decided to rewrite and re-shoot the rest of the footage, this time with sound. The ideal man to help him seemed to be James Whale, a British veteran of the Great War with years of stage experience, now famous for directing the incomparable *Journey's End*. Whale was flattered and excited by the prospect of working with the eccentric Hughes, but production delays kept him away from *Hell's Angels* for some while. In the meantime, Gilbert Miller invited him to Chicago to direct a new company in *Journey's End* and *A Hundred Years Old*, another play by the Quintero brothers.

On Whale's return to Hollywood, Hughes engaged screenwriter Joseph Moncure March to completely rewrite *Hell's Angels*. March found the original silent 'depressingly bad', and set to work on a story which could still incorporate the all-important aerial shots:

> Whale gave me the advice and encouragement I needed and let me work it out the way I wanted. I completed a first draft of the script in ten days and, although some revisions and elaborations were subsequently made, the screenplay stayed essentially the way it was from then on. Hughes and Whale liked the result, and I was asked to stay and work with them [5] . . .

Ben Lyon and James Hall were retained from the original, but Greta Nissen became another victim of the talkies. Her Swedish accent was so strong that the part had to be recast. After several names had been suggested, including *The Love Doctor*'s June Collyer and Carole Peters (later Lombard), Hughes agreed to look at an obscure blonde named Jean Harlow.

Harlow was nervous and apt to be difficult. Whale, exhausted by the crassness of the whole project, wanted only to take his money and be done with the picture. The complete control he would soon have over *Journey's End* must have seemed extremely alluring. March remembered how the director's relations with Harlow became increasingly strained:

> Harlow was quite aware of her deficiencies, and a lot of it must have seemed like a nightmare to her. Even her ability to be seductive was questioned, and in one scene which demanded considerable allure, she could not seem to please Mr Whale. 'Tell me,' she said, with desperate earnestness, 'tell me exactly how you want me to do it.' Mr Whale, his patience sorely tried, said, 'My dear girl, I can tell you how to be an actress but I cannot tell you how to be a woman.'[6]

Whale struggled on and Harlow's performance improved sufficiently for him to re-shoot some of her earlier scenes.

Adding to his workload were the rehearsals and preparations for *Journey's End*, which would now definitely be shot at Tiffany's new studios on Sunset Boulevard. The long, tiring sessions of auditioning and interviewing were undertaken with the film's co-producer George Pearson, who established an office on the lot of Hughes's Metropolitan studio. Whale and Pearson worked well together, but casting proved difficult. Whale was willing to accept any of the various stage casts in their entirety, but this would have caused all kinds of contractual and availability problems.

Slowly the cast came together. The screenplay, however, was a different matter. Both Whale and Maurice Browne had completely rejected V Gareth Gundrey's script, and George Pearson searched around for someone else who could do the play justice. 'Gundrey's script had excellent points,' wrote Pearson, 'technically it was well made, but I felt it over-elaborated much that only needed the utter simplicity of the play. To my mind, the stark realism of *Journey's*

End was due to Sherriff's observation of life, rather than its dissection.'[7]

Someone whom Whale liked and admired was *Hell's Angels* screenwriter Joseph Moncure March, and Whale talked to Pearson about the possibility of March writing the screenplay. Pearson agreed but March was under contract to Howard Hughes, and the director refused to consider loaning him out. Eventually, a compromise was reached which kept Whale on *Hell's Angels* an extra four days. Whale, who had been due to wash his hands of the whole white elephant on Hallowe'en 1929, was frustrated but agreed.

March began work at once, with Whale and Pearson contributing their thoughts on the treatment of the play. As Whale told the *Daily Mail*, he had waged

> a successful battle to pilot the play through the maze of Hollywood conventions which were threatening to rob the film of its atmosphere. 'There was plenty of tact and firmness needed before we started. Mr George Pearson, who supervised the production, and I found that Hollywood had quite made up their minds about what the screen version was going to be like – with a love interest, charming English scenery, and the usual war-film conventions all thrown in. We held out for our own scenario and our own methods – and were finally given our way amid many dubious head-shakings and general pessimism.

After supervising the post-production of *Hell's Angels*, Whale was finally free to concentrate on *Journey's End* by 4 November 1929. The ever-bountiful Hughes gave him a $5000 bonus as a thankyou. Whale bought a Chrysler with the money and told his friends that it was a gift from Hughes.

The *Journey's End* cast was now complete, with one major exception. Just as before, the company found themselves without a Captain Stanhope. Pearson suggested contacting Laurence Olivier, but Whale could no longer be content with the slickness of his performance after the repressed hysteria Colin Clive had brought to the role. Therefore, Whale and Pearson urgently began to press

Maurice Browne to loan out Clive from the London production. This was bound to lead to complications. Sherriff, who was by now being introduced to Kipling, Churchill and the King as well as presenting the play's original manuscript to the League of Nations, was particularly worried:

> I went to Maurice Browne and begged him not to let Clive go. Clive had been the outstanding success of the play. The romantic attraction of a young actor who had found stardom in a night still drew the crowds, and his performance had developed and matured. To take him away would knock out the keystone that held the play together. . . .
>
> Maurice Browne insisted that I was grossly exaggerating Clive's importance. People came to see the play, not individuals in it. He pointed out that it was filling theatres everywhere it went, regardless of what actor played the leading part. In any case, he said, Clive would only be away for a month. He would be back for the anniversary performance, and no possible harm done.[8]

Clive was in fact to be away for eight weeks. He boarded the *Homeric* at Southampton, arriving in New York with just twenty minutes to get to Grand Central Station and catch his train to Los Angeles. Exhausted, he arrived at the Sunset Boulevard studios and did his first voice test, which George Pearson described as 'an inarticulate grumble'.

After the sound problems were sorted out, Whale finally had his team together. He set out his ideas for the piece in an interview with the *New York Times* just before filming commenced:

> When it comes to human emotions, people are exactly the same . . . and the simpler a big situation is presented to them the harder it strikes. The whole foundation of *Journey's End*, to my mind, is that it presents an unusual situation in a most appealing way. Some critics have said that it violates the ethics of the drama. It does not, because the essential element in all drama is truth.[9]

It was a fascinating cast. The Canadian David Manners, cousin to Lady Diana Cooper, became the new Raleigh; Billy Bevan, who played Trotter, had been a comedian with Mack Sennett; Tom Whitely, the sergeant-major, had been the last passenger to leave the *Titanic* alive; and Anthony Bushell, who played the cowardly Hibbert, would later find fame as Olivier's co-producer on *Richard III*. Bushell was filled with admiration for the novice Whale's approach:

> James faced the whole set-up with a quiet and implacable determination that the only way to make the film was his way, and that he was going to get it. To start with, he refused even to consider shooting unless Colin Clive was made available to play Stanhope ... in his quiet, inexorable way, he got him in the end. Next, he demanded from his astonished producers two weeks rehearsal with the full cast before a camera turned ... James got his rehearsal time. Everything of course depended on how James would tackle the actual shooting. ... No fuss, no hesitation, no intimidation by his technicians – he might have been directing talking pictures all his working life. His control of actors was very severe, but he always knew he was right. Never forget he was a damned good actor himself.[10]

Whale was clearly in control and determined to demonstrate his abilities. Working closely with his cameraman Benjamin Kline and the much more experienced Pearson, shooting advanced steadily. Pearson was impressed:

> He had a habit of sitting with one foot tucked under him, perfectly still, eyes intent, ears alert for any error in emphasis or inflection. These were really stage rehearsals, unimpeded by camera technique, in order that the players would be word and action perfect when the filming began, and a translation of a play to the screen called for new conventions. The moment arrived after three days of stage rehearsals.
>
> Filming started. Whale was as determined as myself that nothing should go wrong. In that intention we discussed the

vital element of camera mobility, and the film's peculiar ability to condense time whereby stage minutes became screen seconds. He was aware of these essentials through his experience in *Hell's Angels*, and so, because of our mutual confidence in each other, all went well. With all the purely technical points agreed, we sat together during filming. When he was satisfied that he had obtained what he wanted by rehearsal, the camera 'take' was made, and during this I retired to the sound-booth to check speech clarity. In this friendly fashion the film was made.[11]

The filming progressed, six days a week with one day off for Christmas. Pearson and Clive decided to make the most of it, and had an adventure which doubtless appealed to Whale's sense of humour:

> Christmas Day arrived ... Hollywood was one mad whirlpool of merrymaking, banners and balloons, woollen snowmen, a Father Christmas at every street corner, crowded saloons, constant health-drinking punctuated with carol singing, strangers shaking hands with strangers and persistent calls of 'Just one for the road'. My mind flew back to England, my wife and my children and I longed to be back with them in a saner English Christmas. ... Colin and I had been invited to [Victor] McLaglen's but in the darkness we lost our Hollywood bearings. ... A brilliantly lit building attracted us. ... A perfect butler opened the door. Colin, who had been a victim of the festivities, was in a deep sleep. The butler said he would fetch his master, an immaculately dressed gentleman of imposing appearance who seemed to be expecting our arrival. He said he was sorry for our sad mission, but that even death can be consoled by reverent obsequies: it was only then that we realized that we had struck a Funeral Parlour.[12]

Clive resumed filming the next day and was finished by 29 December, after which he raced back to London. 'By Jove,' he told *The Times*, 'people earn their money out there. Everywhere the

English actor is wanted, and there is immense opportunity in the new "talkie" field.' Unfortunately, R C Sherriff's predictions about Clive's importance proved correct and the *Journey's End* phenomenon began to die down. Attendances had dropped during Clive's absence and, when he returned from filming, the spell was broken.

It was inevitable that such an extraordinary time couldn't last for ever, but all concerned had done remarkably well out of it. Sherriff had earned £48,000 in royalties from the worldwide performance rights and the published version, which had sold 175,000 copies. A South African restaurateur had even written, requesting permission to name his new eaterie after the play. Sherriff assented but concluded that if the food inside were as delectable as the enclosed photograph of the restaurant, then the new name 'held a grim significance for those who went to eat there'.

James Whale, of course, was far away from the winding down of the original London production. His film of the play was finished and edited by 9 March 1930, and received its premiere in Glendale on 13 March.

Journey's End remains a considerable achievement for a first-time film director. Whale managed to open out the action of the stage play without compromising the tightness of the original script. His approach is restrained and a little too careful, particularly his preservation of the proscenium arch, but his camerawork is fluid and interesting. The battle scenes, which are the chief cinematic invention of the piece, are vivid and different. It is clear that Whale was excited by the possibilities of new film techniques and determined to master the medium quickly.

Several of Whale's favourite film conventions are established in *Journey's End*, particularly his device of introducing a character in darkness, moving into light, and building up their mystique via descriptive dialogue. The heroic Stanhope, after all the fulsome praise of his men ('The finest officer in the battalion'), wanders into the dugout with his only thought for whisky.

Much has also been made of an apparent gay subtext in *Journey's End*. As the film follows the play so closely, it is more fruitful to look for evidence of this in Sherriff's play than in any perceived input from Whale.

Sherriff was an interesting man who never married and who remained devoted to his mother throughout his life. His autobiography is entitled, tantalizingly, *No Leading Lady*, though this refers directly to *Journey's End*'s unfashionable absence of a female character, one of the elements it was thought would guarantee failure on its first production. Sherriff's clear identification with manly pursuits, such as his beloved rowing club, belies his obvious affinity with a rather tender masculine bonding. Stanhope's relationship with the character of Osborne, lovingly referred to as 'Uncle', is affecting and genuine, even extending to a scene in which 'Uncle' puts Stanhope to bed:

Stanhope: Dear old Uncle, tuck me up! Kiss me Uncle!

Osborne: Kiss you be hanged. You go to sleep.

While there is an obvious comradely banter in this exchange, the level of the men's intimacy is interesting. 'Uncle' even responds angrily to another's criticism of the alcoholic Stanhope:

Osborne: He's by far the best company Commander we've got. . . .You don't know him as I do. I love that fellow. I'd go to hell with him.

Captain: Oh, you sweet, sentimental old darling.

When Osborne is killed in a raid, Stanhope's outburst against the naive newcomer Raleigh is extraordinarily hysterical:

Stanhope: The one man I could trust. My best friend. The one man I could talk to as man to man. Who understood *everything*. And you think I don't care. . . . You forget. You little fool. You forget. Don't you understand? You forget. Do you think there's a limit to what a man can bear?

Colin Clive's performance adds enormously to this outburst, making it 'more like the grief of a lover than a friend'.[13] Clive was bisexual and part of his drinking problem may have stemmed from his inability to come to terms with this aspect of his character. David

Manners, who played Raleigh, remembered the brilliant Clive and the ragged, histrionic performance he gave in the film:

> To me, his face was a tragic mask. I know he was a tortured man. There seemed to be a split in his personality: one side that was soft, kind and gentle; the other, a man who took to alcohol to hide from the world his true nature. ... Today he would find help. Everyone of us wanted to help then, but when he was on the bottle, which was most of the time, he put on the mask of a person who repelled help and jeered at his own softness. He was a fantastically sensitive actor – and, as with many great actors, this sensitivity bred addiction to drugs or alcohol in order to cope with the very insensitive world around them.[14]

James Whale coaxed Clive into a brilliant performance, using the actor's own insecurities to great effect in the creation of Stanhope. In the final scene, Clive nurses the dying Manners in a particularly tender and sensitive moment. There is nothing implicitly gay in this, but Whale achieves an exquisite tenderness in the relationships between his male characters.

The critics raved about *Journey's End*. The *Los Angeles Examiner*'s fearsome Louella Parsons thought the film

> So perfect in construction, so delicate in thought, so deftly directed and so admirably played ... that we pause for adjectives sufficiently strong to express our appreciation. We grow cold when we think how clumsily this great war play by R C Sherriff might have been put on the screen.

There was also great praise for the performances, particularly Clive, Ian MacLaren and Anthony Bushell, but some dispute over the relative merits of the stage and screen versions. The *Literary Digest* thought Clive

> a fine, honest and thrilling player who looks something like Walter Huston. It seems to me, however, that he possesses a certain stolidness that fails to show the tragic touch of

neurotic, sentimental weakness that makes Stanhope so poignant and touching a character. Therefore, he is less moving in the part than is Colin Keith-Johnstone of the New York stage company. Ian MacLaren is a perfect Osborne, every bit as good as is Leon Quartermaine, of the Broadway version, and Anthony Bushell makes the weakling Hibbert less pathological than does Jack Hawkins on stage.

Whale was singled out for praise, both for the fluidity of his direction and for resisting the temptation to open the play out too much. The *Film Spectator* found Whale's direction commendable, but regretted his fondness for close-ups which, it felt, blotted out the authentic war background. *Variety* concluded that if the English could leave their talking pictures in the hands of Whale and Pearson then they would achieve worldwide distribution. Clearly delighted, Whale told the *Daily Mail*:

> Now that the result has been shown, the film people there – as always – have been most generous in their admission that they were wrong. The triumph which has greeted our flouting of the accepted conventions has been so decided that it has left us gasping a little.

Notes

1. R C Sherriff, *No Leading Lady* (London: Victor Gollancz, 1968), p. 142.
2. Ibid., p. 148.
3. Sheridan Morley, *Tales from the Hollywood Raj* (London: Weidenfeld & Nicolson, 1983).
4. Michael Balcon, *A Lifetime of Films* (London: Hutchinson, 1969).
5. Joseph Moncure March, *Look*, letter, New York, March 1954.
6. Ibid.
7. George Pearson, *Flashback* (London: Allen & Unwin, 1957).
8. Sherriff, *No Leading Lady*, p. 190.
9. Interview with James Whale, *New York Times*, 8 September 1929; quoted in Paul Jensen, *Film Comment*, spring 1971.

10. Anthony Bushell, Arts Lab Programme – Oct/Dec, 1981. The Arts
     Lab Programme was produced to accompany a short retrospective
     of Whale's films.
11. Pearson, *Flashback*.
12. Ibid.
13. Stephen Bourne, 'Hollywood's gay auteur' (unpublished thesis),
     London College of Printing, 1988.
14. David Manners, interview with Gregory Mank, Los Angeles, 1976;
     quoted in *Frankenstein* script book (New Jersey: Magic Image Film
     Books, 1989).

Chapter five

IT seemed as if Whale's passage to major-league direction would be smooth following the success of *Journey's End*, but this proved not to be so. He signed up with Rudolph Valentino's former agent S George Ullman, who proposed that Whale should make himself somewhat more elusive in order to create interest in him. As a result, Whale left Hollywood, firstly for New York, where he arranged to direct another *Journey's End* company for Gilbert Miller, and thence back to England where he had agreed to direct R C Sherriff's much anticipated follow-up to *Journey's End, Badger's Green*. If Whale was concerned that the industry wasn't breaking down his door with offers of work, he didn't show it. He was still interested in dividing his time between stage and screen and would go with the flow. However, something else had arisen which was likely to bring him back to Hollywood sooner rather than later.

David Lewis was an exceptionally handsome young man of twenty-six who had come to Hollywood after bronchial problems curtailed his acting career. He had some friends and good contacts in the film industry and eventually landed a job as assistant story editor to Eddie Montagne at Paramount.

It was in June 1929 that Lewis got a call from Mary Alice Scully, a friend and literary agent who was arranging James Whale's trip to California and had found accommodation for him at the Villa Carlotta. She asked if Lewis would do her a big favour and take the new director out to lunch. Whale arrived, tired and quiet after the endless rail journey across America. Lewis took him to a restaurant called Madame Helen's, where they dined with producer Bud Lighton. Conversation was minimal. Whale's natural reserve was exacerbated by the long journey and the unfamiliarity of his surroundings. As they parted, Lewis advised Whale to save his money, which Whale assured him he would.

However formal the events of that first meeting had been, the two men liked each other and were both gay. Tired and uncommunicative as he was, Whale must have perked up at the sight of the attractive Lewis. The fourteen years which separated them was, of course, no obstacle to a man of Whale's tastes.

After the initial lunch, they met again briefly at a Paramount screening and began to see each other regularly. This soon progressed to a nightly dinner at the famous Brown Derby on Vine, where Whale indulged in steak and the two discussed the problems of *Journey's End*, which was soon to start filming. (Whale even tested Lewis for the part of Hibbert, but it was not a success.) Whatever their professional relations, the two men were falling in love. Whale must have felt torn, then, when he returned to England in April 1930 to direct *Badger's Green*.

All concerned were expecting Sherriff to come up with another *Journey's End*. What about an epic concerning the crew of a doomed submarine at the bottom of the sea? Scott of the Antarctic? Miners buried beneath the earth? The Black Hole of Calcutta? Advice from friends and fans was diverse and, mostly, ludicrous. What Sherriff wanted more than anything was to prove his versatility by doing something completely different. After two years with *Journey's End* and *Hell's Angels*, Whale felt just the same.

The problem for Sherriff, however, lay not only in subject matter but in confidence. He was haunted by the idea that he had only one story in him. He knew about life in the trenches but, outside of that, his experience was limited. One story from his old days at the rowing club appealed to him, however, as its portrayal of village life was familiar to him. The play that he conceived from the bare bones of this original story concerned a village called Badger's Green which is threatened by developers. A lengthy cricket match formed the crux of the piece.

Maurice Browne, who would again produce, was disappointed that Sherriff hadn't come up with a new *Journey's End*, but agreed that it was wise to try something very different. Sherriff sent an outline to Whale while the latter was still in

Hollywood, and Whale agreed to direct the play as soon as *Journey's End* came off at the Prince of Wales.

Unsurprisingly, a great many famous names found themselves unexpectedly available for the new play, hoping that Sherriff could bring off the same trick twice and guarantee them success and a long spell of work. Whale succeeded in luring the respected character actor Horace Hodges into the part of the village doctor and Felix Aylmer for the role of Mr Butler. Sherriff recalled Whale's talent for casting the right actors:

> None of the other parts demanded stars, but there were first-class actors and actresses for them all. Whale had an instinct for finding the right people, and after the first reading I could say to him, as I did after the first reading of *Journey's End*, that he'd got together a perfect team.[1]

As the play was to follow *Journey's End*, principal rehearsals took place, poignantly, on the dugout set. The days passed and rehearsals went very well. Everyone thought it would be just as big a hit, in its way, as the war play.

Finally, the night came for *Journey's End* to bow out. At the final performance, the actors were called before the curtain and cheered. Colin Clive made a thankyou speech, and then the entire company had a party. Maurice Browne's speech reduced him to tears. Everyone was very emotional. Whale was staying with Sherriff in the new house he had bought with his mother:

> We drove home together but neither of us had much to say. We had been through the thing together from the start, and shared all its anxieties, hopes and triumphs. We were both feeling the emptiness it had left behind – far more than we had expected, far more than we allowed ourselves to admit.[2]

Despite their confidence in the new play, *Badger's Green* was not a success. The first-night audience seemed to have a wonderful time and James Agate ran after Sherriff as the playwright left the theatre exclaiming, 'I think you've just made it. I think you've just got away with it. I hope so. Good luck!' Troubled by Agate's words, the formerly confident Sherriff spent a restless night.

The next day's papers confirmed his fears. The critics could only say that it wasn't another *Journey's End*, and that was enough to finish it off. 'SHERRIFF TRIES AGAIN AND FAILS,' wrote Hannen Swaffer. 'Last night we witnessed a play called *Badger's Green*. A play that, but for the acclaim of *Journey's End*, would never have found a place beyond a suburban church hall.'[3] While Whale and Browne were philosophical Sherriff was devastated, and it was some time before he felt able to write again.

In the meantime, Whale was due back in New York to fulfil his obligation to Gilbert Miller's new *Journey's End* company. Things must have appeared far rosier for him than the demoralized Sherriff, but events were to take a strangely similar course. Although well received, the New York *Journey's End* had come to the end of its natural life, and finished after a month. The two one-act comedies which Whale directed as a replacement, Molnár's *The Violet* and *One, Two, Three!* also failed to impress. Thus, Whale found himself heading back to Hollywood and a reunion with David Lewis, but with a rather uncertain future.

On the strength of his *Journey's End* film, Tiffany had offered him a two-picture deal at $20,000 a time. Whale was all-too painfully aware that he was worth a great deal more. He found solace in his blossoming relationship with David Lewis, and they moved into an apartment together at 4565 Dundee Drive. Lewis used his position in the industry to test the water for his lover and found that though *Journey's End* had been very much admired, its stage origins militated against its director being trusted with a proper picture deal.

Bereft of other offers, Whale accepted the contract at Tiffany and opened an office on the lot. He was depressed by the paucity of available properties and though several pictures were announced for him, nothing really took his fancy. These included *The Unpardonable Sin* by Robert Hughes, *X Marks the Spot* by Jack Natteford and Edward T Lowe, and an unnamed gangster project for which Whale posed for pictures with the reknowned mob-exposing author Edward Dean Sullivan. How close any of these projects came to fruition is unknown. Tiffany was strapped for cash and seemed content to announce projects in the hope that they would somehow get started.

Whale was frustrated and demoralized. It was like the early situation with the Stage Society all over again. He had triumphed with *Journey's End* in the West End, Broadway and Hollywood, but no one seemed interested in him. What was needed was another Maurice Browne figure to risk hiring him for a major movie deal. This elusive person finally emerged in early 1931 in the diminutive form of the man who had offered R C Sherriff the screenplay of *All Quiet on the Western Front*, Carl Laemmle Junior.

Laemmle's father, Carl Laemmle *Senior* was a tiny immigrant from Laupheim, Bavaria who, after tiring of the clothing business he ran in Oshkosh, Wisconsin had founded the Universal Film Manufacturing Company in New York in 1912. After two years in production, Laemmle was able to pay $165,000 for 230 acres of the San Fernando Valley, and on 15 March 1915 opened Universal City, California. With typical Laemmle *brouhaha*, the crowd which surged through the newly opened gates sang the 'Star-Spangled Banner', cowboys rode through the streets firing six-guns, a reservoir was dynamited and a rodeo and ball topped off the celebrations. Laemmle's speech ended with the curiously uninspiring words, 'I hope I didn't make a mistake in coming out here.'

By the early 1930s, Universal had become a powerful player in the film industry, though distinctly middle-rank. Some of its hits included Lon Chaney Snr's *Phantom of the Opera* (1925) and *The Hunchback of Notre Dame* (1923), Von Stroheim's *Foolish Wives* (1921), and a seemingly unending diet of cheap programmers and Westerns.

At the age of sixty-four, the diminutive Laemmle, proclaimed by his studio as the 'Prophet of the Picture World', controlled his eccentric empire with a kind of benevolent dictatorship. He loved to be known as 'Uncle Carl' and his nepotism was legendary, as the poet Ogden Nash acidly observed: 'Carl Laemmle had a very large faemmle'. Over seventy relatives, friends and hangers-on, many of whom couldn't even speak English, were on the studio payroll.

Shirley Ulmer, who was briefly married to Laemmle's nephew Max, remembered the extraordinary studio with affection:

> Universal was an eccentric studio and Uncle Carl was an eccentric, dear, crazy old man – let's face it! When we arrived at work in the morning, there was a big billboard as we entered the studio and there would be the motif of the week – 'Be Kind to Others – signed Carl Laemmle', or some beautiful little sentimental message. Every Monday morning it was changed.
>
> It was amazing! At the big Laemmle estate in Benedict Canyon, every Sunday, we all came into the dining room, maybe twenty-four strong – all relatives. And we were not allowed to speak or sit until Uncle Carl made his entrance.[4]

Laemmle had a gift for spotting talent (he gave the legendary Irving Thalberg his first job), but a weakness as far as his own flesh and blood were concerned. So it was that on 28 April 1929 he made his only son Julius (known as 'Junior') general studio manager at the ripe old age of twenty-one.

Junior scored an immediate hit with his first production, the aforementioned *All Quiet on the Western Front*, which had been known around the studio as 'Junior's End'. Against all the odds, it was to triumph and take the Oscar for best picture. Its producer, as tiny as his father, was a cripplingly shy hypochondriac who was totally dominated by Laemmle Senior. Yet he was to produce some of the most interesting and successful films of the 1930s. Shirley Ulmer again:

> A very sensitive human being, a poor, sickly boy and a very sad boy. .... As a producer, he may not have been creative within himself, but he could put a package together. He knew about casting, he knew who could direct.[5]

Indeed, it was seeing the stage version of *Journey's End* which had been instrumental in Laemmle's decision to film *All Quiet*. With his film placed at number two on the *New York Times* Ten Best list of 1930, and *Journey's End* at number three, Junior Laemmle knew where to turn for the directing talent his successful producership would require.

Laemmle had a project immediately in mind for James Whale: Robert E Sherwood's play *Waterloo Bridge*, which the studio had bought after a disappointingly short run on Broadway. The only director whom Junior Laemmle felt could handle the piece was Universal's 'Ace', John Stahl, but he was busy preparing *Strictly Dishonourable*. Whale was a natural second choice, and Laemmle called the English newcomer into his office for an initial meeting. The two got on famously, and Laemmle offered Whale a five-year contract. Whale was delighted to be given a *real* picture and a *real* deal, but he remained bound to his association with Tiffany. Simultaneously, both Tiffany and Universal announced that Whale would soon begin work for them.

The situation was resolved, however, by Whale's attorney, Walter E Burke, who soon found a way out of the situation. It transpired that Whale had been underpaid for his work on *Journey's End* by some $12,998; he sought damages in the Superior Court, and a settlement agreeable to both sides was reached. Whale dropped his case and Tiffany released him from his contract. Finally free to work for Laemmle, Whale signed his forty-weeks-a-year contract at $2500 a week and began shooting *Waterloo Bridge* on 23 May 1931.

Whale chose his friend Benn Levy, who had adapted *Portrait of a Man with Red Hair*, to flesh out Sherwood's two-act play into a screenplay. The story concerned an injured Canadian soldier, Roy Cronin, who meets Myra, a prostitute, during a First World War air raid over Waterloo Bridge. Roy falls in love with Myra and even takes her home to meet his parents, but the relationship is doomed. Myra cannot change her ways. Roy returns to the war, and Myra is apparently killed when a bomb hits the bridge.

For the role of the sensitive Roy, Whale chose the handsome gay actor Kent Douglass (later to change his name to Douglass Montgomery), and for Myra, the exceptionally underrated actress Mae Clarke:

I think Whale saw something I know I had then and that is a basic confusion and insecurity I didn't mind projecting and putting into my work. It would give a little timidity to a scene that would normally have a lot of bite in it, and I think that might be what he saw in me.[6]

Clarke's wonderfully naturalistic performance is one of the film's many surprises. Whale always had a natural affinity with society's outsiders and outcasts, among whose number he could count himself. It is Stanhope who fascinates his camera in *Journey's End* and, naturally, it is Myra the cynical prostitute upon whom he lavishes his attention in *Waterloo Bridge*. The advances Whale had made from the relatively static *Journey's End* are remarkable. It was as if he had become fully conversant with the available technology and mastered it at a stroke.

The film begins with a long tracking shot past the chorus line of the musical in which Myra earns her legitimate living. She stands out at once: while the other girls warble the closing bars of the finale, Myra is yawning and mouthing, amusedly. We follow her to her seedy lodgings, so authentic in their Britishness and their squalor that Whale's hand is obvious. He knew such places only too well, and brings a touch of genuineness to the realization of their atmosphere. Memorable details include the fish supper Roy and Myra enjoy and the utterly relaxed Mae Clarke, who picks pieces of stray tobacco from her tongue as another cheap cigarette disintegrates in her mouth.

There is delightful comedy from Douglass's deaf father, played by veteran Frederick Kerr, and an appealing performance from the then unknown *ingénue* Bette Davis. Kent Douglass is fine and extremely touching as he realizes his love for Myra cannot be reciprocated. It is Clarke's extraordinary performance, however, which lingers in the memory. Through the tremendous vitality of Whale's direction, it is she, rather than Douglass, who carries the film. In her mannerisms, her strength, her independence and perhaps even her lack of real emotion, Myra is more like a man than a woman. In contrast, it is Douglass's Roy who comes closer to the traditional depiction of the female.

Mae Clarke (later to become famous as the girl into whose face James Cagney squashes a grapefruit in *The Public Enemy*) was to make three pictures with Whale. She remembered him with adoration as the most gifted director with whom she ever worked: 'James Whale. He is a giant to me. Always he was the plu-perfect gentleman, and not only that, the *genius*.'[7] She vividly recalled the final scene of the film, an extraordinary crane shot down the length of the bridge as the Zeppelin droned ominously above it:

> The feeling of that scene was so overpowering! Everyone felt a reality over pretense. By that time, we had all learned to take advantage of every second Mr Whale could give us – because his finger and his mind were in every single facet of the production. You'd ask, 'Where is Mr Whale?' 'Oh, he's up on the boom crane tower, creating the bomber effect.' (He wanted to see Myra from the bomber's point of view). You'd ask, 'Where's Mr Whale now?' 'Oh, he's checking the sound.' He knew just where he wanted the shadows ... everything. It was *his* picture: a James Whale Production![8]

Robert Sherwood was equally delighted with the film, and graciously stated that it significantly improved on his original.

Whale brought the film in $25,000 under budget and inside the allotted schedule of twenty-six days. The film premiered at the RKO Orpheum in Los Angeles to very warm reviews. Mordaunt Hall wrote in the *New York Times*:

> Considering the scarcity of opportunities, Mr Whale has done excellent work on the film. ... To impress one with the idea that Roy and Myra are in the country, he gives familiar barnyard noises, such as the crowing of a rooster or the mooing of a cow. When the soldier and the girl are in her dismal abode, one hears the vaguest suggestion of a regimental band passing in a distant thoroughfare.

Like Whale's *Showboat* (1936), the tragedy is that a later, inferior remake has all but buried *Waterloo Bridge*. The 1940 Mervyn Le Roy version starring Robert Taylor was immensely successful but lacks the unsentimental vision of Whale's original.

Junior Laemmle was extremely impressed with the finished result and offered Whale the pick of about thirty available properties. Only one really took Whale's fancy, a story so strange and dark that it must have seemed like a gift to him: *Frankenstein*.

Notes

1. R C Sherriff, *No Leading Lady* (London: Victor Gollancz, 1968), p. 197.
2. Ibid.
3. Hannen Swaffer, quoted in R C Sherriff, *No Leading Lady*.
4. Shirley Ulmer, interview with Gregory Mank; quoted in *Frankenstein* script book (New Jersey: Magic Image Film Books, 1989).
5. Ibid.
6. Art Ronnie, 'Frankenstein Revisited', *Southland Sunday*, December 1971.
7. Mae Clarke, interview with Gregory Mank; quoted in *Frankenstein* script book.
8. Ibid.

Chapter six

IT was on St Valentine's Day, 1931, that Universal released the first of the talking pictures with which it was to become associated for most of the 1930s and 1940s: the horror film. *Dracula*, based on the stage play by Hamilton Deane and starring Bela Lugosi, was an immediate hit and Junior Laemmle's second smash, bringing in receipts of $500,000. Tod Browning's film is a stodgy, rather boring affair but it was a sensation in its day and made Universal acutely aware of the money to be made from frightening the public. Their original horror star, Lon Chaney, had died the year before and Lugosi seemed the natural man to fill his shoes. He did, however, find himself the victim of familiar Laemmle methods before finally winning the part:

> Who was tested? The cousins and brother-in-laws [*sic*] of the Laemmles – all their pets and the pets of their pets! This goes on for a long time and then old man Laemmle says, 'There's nobody in the family that can play it, so why don't we hire an actor?'[1]

Despite having created the role on the stage, Lugosi was only chosen after Ian Keith, Conrad Veidt, Paul Muni and William Courtney had been rejected. It was to be the first in a long line of bruising and hurtful humiliations for the Hungarian actor.

With the receipts from *Dracula* helping to stave off financial crisis (the Laemmles laid off 350 employees in March 1931), Junior was desperate to find a suitable follow-up. Richard L Shayer, head of Universal's story department already had *Frankenstein* up and running as a viable product in association with his friend, the enigmatic French director Robert Florey. Florey, who had worked, among other things, as Rudolph Valentino's advance manager, Hollywood correspondent for the French *Cinemagazine*, foreign publicity director for Pickfair and director of the 1929 *The Hole in the Wall* (debuting Edward G Robinson and Claudette Colbert), as well as the first Marx Brothers feature *The Coconuts* (1929), found himself called in to see the boss. He later recalled the bizarre interview he had with Laemmle:

> The crimes committed by the Monster were relatively easy to imagine and during an unusual interview while Carl Laemmle Jnr surrendered his fingers to a manicurist, his hair to a barber, his thoughts to his secretaries, and his voice to a dictaphone, I explained the general plan of the film to him. He told me to type up the story right away and send it to the head of the scenario department.[2]

Florey and Shayer discussed the *Dracula* follow-up over lunch at the Musso and Frank restaurant, where they considered everything from Poe's *Murders in the Rue Morgue* and Wells's *The Invisible Man* to the Grand Guignol plays of Florey's native France which, ironically, Florey had worked on in Paris just as Whale had in London. Finally, the two men decided that *Frankenstein* offered the best opportunities as a film, and began to thrash out a way of transferring Mary Shelley's 'Modern Prometheus' to the screen. Florey's synopsis lost much of the novel's subtlety, turning Shelley's driven Dr Frankenstein into a two-dimensional mad scientist, and the eloquent monster into a rampaging beast. Nevertheless, it met with Shayer's approval, as Florey recalled: 'Shayer agreed with my conception of the film and told me to go ahead with an extended and detailed adaptation – adding that the front office would insist on Lugosi playing the part of the Monster.'[3] Lugosi was outraged. He had expected to play the part of the *creator*, and complained that the Monster's role could be taken by 'any half-wit', which was certainly true of Florey's version.

While Lugosi brooded, further problems loomed for Robert Florey. Universal purchased the rights to Peggy Webling's play of *Frankenstein* for $20,000. Strangely, the contract stated that part of the fee should go to the writer John Lloyd Balderston, who had commissioned Peggy Webling to adapt the book in the first place. Balderston had co-authored the play of *Dracula* on which Universal's version was based, and was later to contribute to *Bride of Frankenstein*, *The Mummy* (1932) and *Mad Love* (1935). The strange part of the agreement was that, for his money, Balderston was to provide a *screenplay* for *Frankenstein*. This was news to Robert Florey. Despite Shayer's reassurances, he refused to continue work on *his* screenplay until Universal had drawn up a proper contract stating that he would write and direct. They did so, but, to his lasting regret and bitterness, Florey failed to read the contract carefully. It stated that he would indeed write and direct *a* film, but not specifically *Frankenstein*.

Blissfully ignorant, Florey conceived a script with Garrett Fort, for which Fort did most of the work. Florey was responsible for the criminal brain being placed in the Monster's skull and the fiery climax at the old mill, which came to him after looking out of his apartment and seeing the windmill logo of the Van de Kamp bakery.

With the script almost completed, Junior Laemmle granted permission for a test to be shot on the sets of *Dracula*. It was delayed for some time as Lugosi's monster make-up – described by the *Los Angeles Record* as 'two or three different colors, stripes, streaks and striations' – melted in the June sunshine. Lugosi was temperamental and arrogant, clashing with Universal's make-up wizard Jack P Pierce over both the look of the Monster and who should apply the make-up.

Florey grew ever more anxious, but shooting of the test of the creation scene finally began on 15 June 1931. Laemmle engaged *Dracula*'s Van Helsing (Edward Van Sloan) and Renfield (Dwight Frye) to play Dr Waldman and Fritz, the hunchbacked assistant. The parts of Victor Moritz and Henry Frankenstein were filled by contract players whose identities have not survived. Florey's friend Paul Ivano shot the two-reel test over two days, minus the complex electrical and sound effects required by the script:

> Universal was running on a shoe-string in those days and they didn't allow me time to properly plan a lighting layout. With a few assistants we rushed onto the old Dracula sets and

found that the only place we could properly light the scenes were [*sic*] from above, due to the Gothic nature of the structure. We placed a few lights behind the pillars. But we still had the shadows of the scaffolding criss-crossing the actors. Also, with the time so limited we had no time to build any tracks for the camera dollys and so the old Mitchell camera was set stationary behind the operating table with Bela lying on it. Behind was the old staircase from Dracula. We followed the extra, portraying Dr Frankenstein, and Dwight Frye down the steps and stopped with the action taking place behind the monster.[4]

Controversy still rages about the test which has, sadly, not survived. Florey would later claim that Lugosi's make-up closely resembled that eventually used in the film. Edward Van Sloan, by contrast, recalled that '[Lugosi's] head was about four times normal size, with a broad wig on it. He had a polished, clay-like skin and looked more like something out of *Babes in Toyland!*'[5] Florey and Ivano did their best, but were not helped by Lugosi's attitude, as Florey recalled:

As I was working with the other actors, during a time when the Monster had not yet 'come to life', Lugosi kept exclaiming, 'Enough is enough'; that he was not going to be a grunting, babbling idiot for anybody, and that any tall extra could be the Monster. 'I was a star in my country, and will not be a scarecrow over here!' he said repeatedly.[6]

The test was finally completed, despite all the problems, and ran for twenty minutes. It was hastened to a screening-room for Junior Laemmle's approval. Here, history provides us with conflicting accounts. Florey and Ivano both insisted that the top-brass reaction was excellent and that all the principal directors on the lot wanted to make *Frankenstein* as a result. The more familiar account states that Junior burst out laughing at Lugosi's appearance and stalked from the room leaving a somewhat shell-shocked Florey in his wake. Then, Lugosi roared 'Ivano! My close-up was *magnificent!*' and gave the cameraman a box of dollar cigars before leaving in turn. Ivano gave the cigars to the hapless Florey, who must have guessed by now that things weren't going his way.

James Whale had by now signed with Myron Selznick, Hollywood's most powerful agent. On a critical high from *Waterloo Bridge*, he was interested to know what his new contract at Universal might bring him. In the event it was Junior Laemmle who, after the Florey test disaster, approached Whale with the script for *Frankenstein*. Anxious to distance himself from any more war films, Whale took to the idea, more especially because it appealed to his bizarre sense of humour and love of the unusual. As his friend Alan Napier explained: 'There was always a touch of the macabre, the sinister, the sadistic about Jimmy, you couldn't get away from it.'[7]

Although he had reservations about the script, Whale took both it and the original Shelley novel home to read thoroughly. David Lewis found both interesting but 'weird'. Whale, however, perhaps remembering his experiences in Grand Guignol, in particular, the plays *After Death* and *Portrait of a Man with Red Hair*, saw distinct possibilities in the project. He later told the *New York Times*:

> I chose *Frankenstein* out of about 30 available stories because it was the strongest meat and gave me a chance to dabble in the macabre. I thought it would be an amusing thing to try and make what everybody knows to be a physical impossibility believable for 60 minutes. A director must be pretty bad if he can't get a thrill out of war, murder, robbery. *Frankenstein* was a sensational story and had a chance to become a sensational picture. It offered fine pictorial possibilities, had 2 grand characterizations, and dealt with a subject which might go anywhere – and that is part of the fun of making pictures.[8]

Laemmle's offer to Whale took no account of Florey's feelings. The outraged Frenchman studied his contract and discovered the unsavoury truth. Dick Shayer, aware of Whale's high status at the studio, advised Florey to begin work on an adaptation of *Murders in the Rue Morgue*. Whale was Laemmle's favourite and if he was interested in *Frankenstein* then Florey might as well forget about it. In the end, both Florey *and* Lugosi were shifted to *Rue Morgue*, leaving Whale with a free hand and Florey with a bitterness he would harbour for the rest of his life.

How much Whale knew of these behind-the-scenes dramas is unclear, but he could be cold and ruthless when necessary. Just as he had wriggled out of his contract with Tiffany, once he had set his heart on *Frankenstein* he was determined to get it, as Alan Napier confirmed: 'Jimmy saw everything in terms of a step up the ladder. He gloried in achieving success.'[9]

Having trounced Florey and now on a par with Universal's top director John Stahl, Whale set about changing *Frankenstein* to suit his tastes. The Florey/Fort script's chief weakness, he felt, was its shallow characterization of the creator and his monster. Whale felt it essential that Frankenstein be more than a mad scientist and that his creation should evoke sympathy as well as horror.

Whale set to work with Garrett Fort and newcomer Francis Edward Faragoh to refashion the script. John Lloyd Balderston's adaptation featured several intriguing episodes not included in the Florey screenplay, and these scenes, including the Monster's meeting with the little girl, were drafted in. Whale screened *The Cabinet of Dr Caligari*, *The Golem* and *Metropolis* to reacquaint himself with the German Expressionism he so admired. In addition, he watched MGM's 1926 silent *The Magician*, which contained the now-familiar elements of a tower laboratory and an evil dwarf assistant. He then set about casting what was to become the most famous horror film of all time.

Frankenstein was the first picture in which Whale could wholly exercise his creative muscle, and he was determined to cast the picture with people whom he liked and respected. Edward Van Sloan and Dwight Frye had acquitted themselves well in Florey's test and would be familiar to the audience from their roles in *Dracula*, so they were kept on. Following her performance in Whale's previous film, the part of Frankenstein's fiancée, Elizabeth, was briefly offered to Bette Davis. Junior Laemmle, however, didn't like her, famously claiming that she had as much sex appeal as Slim Summerville! Whale acquiesced and instead selected Mae Clarke who had done such fine work for him as Myra in *Waterloo Bridge*.

'I asked for Mae Clarke', said Whale, 'because of her intelligence, fervour, and sincere belief that *Frankenstein* would claim the public's interest.'[10]

Whale beefed up her part, crucially placing her in the creation sequence, for example, and assured Clarke that she wouldn't be out of place in the predominantly European cast:

> When we had our first rehearsal meeting, I said, 'Really? British Lady Elizabeth?' Mr Whale said, 'I think so. We don't have to go in for the broad "A" – just a word here and there for flavouring.' I worried about the English accent, but finally Mr Whale said, 'When you speak remember to cross your "t's". ... As it developed, the part of Elizabeth was not a good follow-up to Myra rolewise, but this was more than compensated for in a continuing association with prestige pictures.[11]

Having settled on Clarke for Elizabeth and stolid leading man John Boles as the pretender to her affections, Victor Moritz, Whale turned his attentions to Dr Henry Frankenstein. Laemmle wanted Leslie Howard, but Whale felt quite rightly that Howard's suaveness would be quite wrong for the role of the driven, nervy scientist. In his mind there was only one man for the job: his friend and 'discovery' Colin Clive.

Since his success in *Journey's End*, Clive had continued to prosper, but was already showing signs of the weariness and crippling inner torment which would destroy him. The Frankenstein Whale envisaged was quite similar to Clive's Captain Stanhope, and he wrote to England requesting that Clive make himself available:

> I chose Colin Clive for *Frankenstein* because he had exactly the right kind of tenacity to go through with anything, together with the kind of romantic quality which makes strong men leave civilization to shoot big game. There is also a level-headedness about Clive which keeps him in full control of himself even in his craziest moments in the picture.[12]

Clive happily accepted, glad to be working with his friend again, and boarded the *Aquitania* for New York. It is clear from Whale's letter to Clive that the two were very much kindred spirits and saw the same prospects in the film:

> It is a grand part and I think will fit you as well as Stanhope. I see Frankenstein as an intensely sane person, at times rather fanatical and in one or two scenes a little hysterical ... Frankenstein's nerves are all to pieces. He is a very strong, extremely dominant personality, sometimes quite strange and queer, sometimes very soft, sympathetic and decidedly romantic ...
>
> There are none of Dracula's maniacal cackles. I want the picture to be a very modern, materialistic treatment of this medieval story – something of *Doctor Caligari*, something of Edgar Allan Poe, and of course a good deal of us ... I know you are absolutely right for it.[13]

Whale also suggested that Clive speak to as many Americans as possible in order to 'loosen' his English accent. At this stage, Whale could promise three days' rehearsal before shooting began and that the script would probably be revised further.

With Clive on board, the only remaining obstacle was the most problematic of all. Who would play the Monster? As Lugosi had pointed out, anyone could have played the part as envisaged by Florey, but Whale's monster was of a different order: a pathetic creature driven to kill by the impulses in its abnormal brain. An actor of rare sensitivity was required, but Whale could think of no one suitable. He came to David Lewis one day and asked his lover for suggestions. Lewis had been impressed by an actor he had seen in Columbia's *The Criminal Code* (1931). His name was Boris Karloff.

Karloff, at forty-three a veteran of countless B pictures, happened to be on the Universal lot making a gangster movie called *Graft*. He was sitting having tea in the commissary when Whale found him:

> [Whale] was lunching at a nearby table. Suddenly he caught my eye and beckoned me over. I leapt – he was the most

important director on the lot. He asked me to sit down. I did, holding my breath, and then he said: 'Your face has startling possibilities ... ' I cast my eyes down modestly, and then he said, 'I'd like you to test for the Monster in *Frankenstein*.' It was shattering – for the first time in my life I had been gainfully employed long enough to buy myself some new clothes and spruce up a bit – actually I rather fancied myself! Now, to hide all this new-found beauty under make-up? I said I'd be delighted.[14]

While Whale toiled on the final draft of the script, Karloff and Jack Pierce worked at night on the Monster's make-up. It was essential to avoid the ludicrous look Lugosi had presented, and Pierce worked assiduously at his task. He reasoned that Frankenstein, a doctor but not a practising surgeon, would take the easiest route in transplanting the stolen organs he used to build his creation. The top of the skull would be sawn off and the new brain popped in, then the bone clamped together. The infamous plugs in the sides of its neck would have acted as electrical conduits:

> I read that the Egyptians used to bind some criminals hand and foot and bury them alive. When their blood turned to water after death, it flowed into their extremities, stretched their arms to gorilla length and swelled their hands, feet and faces to abnormal proportions. I thought this might make a nice touch for the Monster, since he was supposed to be made from the corpses of executed felons – I made his arms look longer by shortening the sleeves of his coat, stiffened his legs with two pairs of pants over steel struts.[15]

After covering Karloff's face in blue-green greasepaint, blackening his fingernails with shoe polish, pinching his cheeks with clamps and adding the incredible thirteen-pound asphalt-spreader's boots, the look was almost ready. Whale was delighted. He had instructed Pierce to create a version according to his own design which gave Karloff bizarre ringed ridges on his forehead and a pendulous lower lip, but this was felt to make the Monster look too evil. Pierce's new version was much more the Monster Whale desired:

Boris Karloff's face has always fascinated me and I made drawings of his head, added sharp bony ridges where I imagined the skull might have been joined. His physique was weaker than I could wish, but that queer, penetrating personality of his, I felt, was more important than his shape, which could easily be altered.[16]

Altered it was, and Karloff had to suffer a double-quilted suit underneath his costume to pad him out. He would arrive for make-up at 4 a.m. and be on set at 9 a.m. At lunchtime, he was unable to eat with the rest of the crew, partly because his make-up was a closely guarded secret and partly because it was easier for him to eat alone. He would strip off his sweat-sodden costume and eat his solitary meal. After going for a wander one day, and making a girl faint, Karloff was forced to wear a blue veil over his face. 'Some of our nice little secretaries are pregnant,' explained Laemmle Snr, 'and they might be frightened if they saw him.'

As shooting neared completion, the incredibly patient Karloff complained that the hours Whale made him work – fifteen or sixteen each day – were more than that allowed by an Academy edict. Whale and the studio conceded, and Karloff was allowed to come to work an hour and a half later. Pierce had, by now, worked out a quicker method of applying and removing the make-up, so the whole process was speeded up somewhat.

Whale was in his stride now, delighted and excited by the possibilities of the new shocker. There were daily tea breaks, which were enjoyed by the predominantly English cast, as Mae Clarke recalled:

The *Frankenstein* set was like a scientist's laboratory – although there were pleasantries. Every day, there was tea time. And everyone on the set had his own cup and saucer (no Dixie cups would do) and little cookies (no 'Danish' please). Cream or lemon – take your choice – and don't forget your serviette (otherwise termed a paper napkin). It was an enjoyable mini-playtime and a novelty for us 'Yanks' – then it was back to 'the Lab' and all business.[17]

With Arthur Edeson on camera and Clarence Kolster editing (both had worked on *Waterloo Bridge*), Whale brought the film in five days over schedule and $30,000 over budget. Mae Clarke concluded: 'From the picture's inception we approached it as a serious work with a serious view. I think this gave it dignity and helped make it a classic.'[18] Bela Lugosi called Karloff with a somewhat different view, however: 'The part's nothing but perhaps it will make you a little money.'[19]

Whale's film eschews the gothic splendour of Shelley's novel in favour of a grim expressionistic feel. It appears to be set at some time in the 1920s, though great pains are made to distance the viewer from thinking of it as reality.

The screenplay called for a lengthy opening sequence showing mourners laboriously carrying a coffin up the hill to the cemetery. Whale shot the sequence, but decided to begin his film with the lowering of the coffin into the grave. He tracks past the line of mourners and a statue of Death, only pausing as Fritz the dwarf hauls himself to his feet. Frankenstein appears at once behind him, rasping 'Down ... down, you fool!' They lie in wait until the coffin is buried and then set to work, disinterring it. As they feverishly dig, Frankenstein shovels a lump of soil straight into the face of the statue of Death. Within a very few moments, Whale has plunged straight into the narrative, establishing his themes and Frankenstein's cavalier attitudes to the power of Death. The scientist caresses the coffin. 'He is just resting, waiting for a new life to come.'

Whale is less comfortable with the romantic interlude between Elizabeth and Victor, though he quickly establishes the triangular conflict between the two and Henry Frankenstein by opening the scene on Frankenstein's portrait and cutting rapidly to close-ups of both Boles and Clarke. Again, Whale makes his point with great economy.

The film moves rapidly to the creation sequence, arguably one of the most famous moments in film history. Consisting of eighty-five cuts, Whale brilliantly constructs a symphony of electrical wonder, courtesy of Kenneth Strickfadden's special effects, as the inert corpse is raised into the lightning-filled sky. Once the

Monster has been brought back to earth, Whale cuts to the tiny flicker of life in its hand, pulling back rapidly to Frankenstein's hysterical cry, 'It's alive! It's alive!'

> Victor: Henry – In the name of God!
>
> Frankenstein: In the name of God? Now I know what it feels like to *be* God!

Whale later described just why he felt this scene was central to the film:

> I consider the creation of the Monster to be the high spot of the film, because if the audience did not believe the thing had been really made, they would not be bothered with what it was supposed to do afterward. To build this up, I showed Frankenstein collecting his material bit by bit. He proves to the audience through his conversation with Professor Waldman that he actually did know something about science, and particularly the ultra-violet ray, from which he was expecting the miracle to happen. He deliberately tells his plan of action. By this time, the audience must at least believe something is going to happen; it might be disaster, but at least they will settle down to see the show.
>
> Frankenstein puts his spectators in their positions, he gives the final orders to Fritz, he turns the levers and sends the diabolic machine soaring upward toward the roof, into the storm. He is now in a state of feverish excitement calculated to carry both the spectators in the windmill and the spectators in the theatre with him. The lightning flashes. The Monster begins to move. Frankenstein merely has to believe what he sees, which is all we ask the audience to do.[20]

Whale's outsider this time is, of course, the Monster, who, like Captain Stanhope, is spoken of before his arrival as Frankenstein and his mentor Dr Waldman discuss the ethics of the experiment. When Waldman reveals for the first time that the Monster possesses a criminal brain, Whale shows us a flicker of doubt in the sideways glance of the formerly confident Frankenstein.

It is enough to suggest the horror of what might come. Suddenly, the Monster is approaching. Frankenstein puts out the lights, ready for a characteristic introduction in darkness. But Whale tantalizes further by having Boris Karloff *back* into the room, and employs another favourite device as he reveals the Monster's face in three jarring close-ups.

The Monster, initially childlike and gentle, is goaded into violence by the vicious Fritz and escapes into the countryside. Here he encounters a little girl, sitting by a lake. Little Maria, played by seven-year-old Marilyn Harris, is tossing flowers into the water and, unafraid of the terrifying Monster, invites him to participate in the game. Delighted, the Monster does so, until he runs out of flowers and, pathetically, throws the little girl into the lake, expecting her to float also. This scene caused the only major upset of the shoot. Boris Karloff recalled the incident:

> Well, that was the only time I didn't like Jimmy Whale's direction. ... My conception of the scene was that [the Monster] would look up at the little girl in bewilderment, and *in his mind*, she would become a flower. Without moving, he would pick her up gently and put her into the water exactly as he had done to the flowers – and, to his horror, she would sink. Well, Jimmy made me pick her up and do THAT (motioning violently) over my head which became a brutal and deliberate act. ... The whole pathos of the scene, to my mind, should have been – and I'm sure that's the way it was written – completely innocent and unaware.[21]

Karloff was convinced that all the sympathy they had struggled so hard to establish would be lost. Whale, however, would have none of it:

> He fumbled for his words as he tried to convey why to us, because in a strange way we were all very hostile about it. He couldn't just bully us into acceptance. Then he said, 'You see, it's all part of the *ritual*'.[22]

The disgruntled Karloff carried on with the scene as Marilyn Harris recalled:

James Whale was very, very sweet – *very* nice. I never saw the
script for *Frankenstein*; he just told me what the scene was
about, and what my lines were. After the Monster threw me
in the lake, I was supposed to swim underwater, but I'd only
had about three swimming lessons – I didn't even know how
to go underwater. They had row-boats in a semi-circle
outside of camera range, in case I got caught in the
undergrowth in the water, so I was fully protected.

But the first time the Monster threw me in, I couldn't
get underwater – I had too many clothes on! I tried to get
under, but I just couldn't, because of the petticoats and
stockings and shoes and what little girls wear ... [23]

Little Miss Harris was ruthlessly controlled by an obnoxious stage-
mother, who was heard to shout after the end of the first take,
'Throw her in again! *Farther*!' Harris recalled how Whale resolved
the problem:

James Whale came over and talked about it. And he said, 'If
you'll do it again, you think about it, and I'll give you
anything you want.' So the second shot went fine ... Whale
came over later and said, 'Now what is it you want?' And I
said, 'A dozen boiled eggs!'[24]

Marilyn's mother was furious that she hadn't asked for something
more expensive, but her diet was rigidly controlled and eggs were
very special to her. In the event, Whale sent her *two* dozen.

Towards the end of the film, the Monster confronts Elizabeth
in her boudoir, as Mae Clarke recalled:

Here's a scene that could have been funny. I'm in my room
dressed in my bridal gown and Henry and I are discussing our
future plans and the Monster. Suddenly we hear the Monster
but Henry isn't quite sure where he is. First he's upstairs.
Then he's in the cellar. Henry just isn't tuned in. Then he
foolishly locks me in for safekeeping while he and the others
search for the Monster. Doesn't he know the Monster could
get in through the window?

Just before filming the confrontation scene between the Monster and myself, Whale said, 'Now we've all read it, let's do the mechanics.' He really directed from inspiration. As the Monster advances toward me, my attention is drawn away every time I am about to turn and see him. Whale milked it carefully. The scene had to be peaked and cut off at just the right moment.

Between Karloff's perfect performance and my throwing myself so thoroughly into the role, I feared I would drop dead. I asked Boris if he knew any tricks that would help me. 'Remember,' he said, 'when I am coming at you keep your eye on my up-camera little finger. I'll keep wiggling it. Then you'll know it's only Boris underneath all this make-up.' Fortunately for me, Boris didn't forget to wiggle his finger.[25]

The film climaxes as the Monster is being chased across the mountains by the inevitable mob of angry villagers and the guilt-stricken Frankenstein. Whale forced Karloff to carry the unconscious Colin Clive up and down the hill set over and over again until he was satisfied, causing the actor great pain. Indeed, their fight sequence proved so brutal that Clive dislocated his arm.

Finally, cornered in a burning windmill, the tragic Monster tosses Frankenstein to the ground and is consumed by the flames. Colin Clive was delighted with this ending and told the *New York Times*:

> I think *Frankenstein* has an intense dramatic quality that continues throughout the play and culminates when I, in the title role, am killed by the Monster that I have created. This is a rather unusual ending for a talking picture, as the producers generally prefer that the play end happily with the hero and heroine clasped in each other's arms.[26]

After some thought, however, Whale decided that Frankenstein should live and filmed an epilogue in which the old Baron stands outside his son's bedroom, surrounded by giggling servants, and proposes a toast: 'Here's to a son to the house of

Frankenstein!' 'This semi-happy ending,' said Whale, 'was added to remind the audience that after all – it is only a tale that is told, and could easily be twisted any way by the director.'[27]

The finished film was a triumphant vindication of Whale's approach. He coaxed a performance from Colin Clive which set the standard for all Hollywood's 'mad' scientists (it was even cited by Peter Cushing as virtually unsurpassable when he came to play his own magnificent Baron Frankenstein in Hammer's 1957 version).

Whale had, of course, written to Clive that *Frankenstein* would contain 'a great deal of us', but what, precisely, did he mean by this? The two men were close friends and obviously had something of a shared vision and world-view. The bisexual Clive, unhappy in a bizarre marriage to the lesbian Jeanne de Casalis, was just as much an outsider as Whale himself, and it is tempting to see Clive as Whale's onscreen counterpart: ambitious, flouting convention, wilfully detached from an all-too straight-laced society. Mae Clarke recalled Clive's qualities as an actor:

> Colin Clive was the dearest, kindest man who gave you importance. He was wonderful, so clever. When he started acting in a scene, I wanted to stop and just watch . . . I'd think 'Here I am, playing scenes with this marvellous actor!' Mr Whale would say, 'Colin's voice is like a pipe organ . . . I just pull out the stops and he produces music'.
>
> Colin was electric. I was mesmerised by him – so much that I hoped it didn't show! When he looked at me, I'd flush. . . . He was the handsomest man I ever saw – and also the saddest. Colin's sadness was elusive; the sadness you see if you contemplate many of the master painters' and sculptors' conceptions of the face of Christ.[28]

This ragged, tragic element, which Whale had first seen in Clive when they worked on *Journey's End*, was further heightened by Whale's direction of *Frankenstein*.

More than anything, however, Whale's *Frankenstein* is justly famous for Boris Karloff's brilliant performance as the Monster. Whale's handling of the misunderstood and brutalized creation lends the performance a poignancy which is lost in almost every other version of the story. Clearly, the director identifies very strongly with the Monster, creating a creature far more complex than the grunting killer of Robert Florey's original screenplay. Instead, in Karloff's sensitive hands, the Monster becomes Whale's *ultimate* outsider: a wholly alienated figure, desiring only love and compassion, and receiving instead rejection at every turn from society's mob. Boris Karloff's words provide a fitting conclusion:

> This was a pathetic creature who, like us all, had neither wish nor say in his creation and certainly did not wish upon itself the hideous image which automatically terrified humans whom it tried to befriend. The most heart-rending aspect of the creature's life, for us, was his ultimate desertion by his creator. It was as though Man, in his blundering, searching attempts to improve himself, was to find himself deserted by his God.[29]

Notes

1. Robert Cremer, *The Man Behind the Cape* (Chicago: Harry Regnery Co., 1976).
2. Robert Florey, *Hollywood: d'hier et d'aujourd'hui* (Paris, 1948).
3. Al Taylor, 'The Forgotten Frankenstein', *Fangoria* 2, October 1979.
4. Paul Ivano, interview with Forrest Ackerman; quoted in *Frankenstein* script book (New Jersey: Magic Image Film Books, 1989).
5. Edward Van Sloan, *Famous Monsters of Filmland*, 31, 1964.
6. Taylor, 'Forgotten Frankenstein'.
7. Alan Napier, interview with Gregory Mank; quoted in *Frankenstein* script book.
8. Interview with James Whale, *New York Times*, quoted in *Frankenstein* script book.
9. Ibid.
10. 'James Whale and Frankenstein', interview, *New York Times*, 20 December 1931.
11. Mae Clarke, interview with Gregory Mank; quoted in *Frankenstein* script book.
12. 'Whale and Frankenstein'.
13. Letter from James Whale to Colin Clive; quoted in 'Frankenstein Finished', *New York Times*, 11 October 1931.

14.   Cynthia Lindsay, *Dear Boris* (New York: Alfred A Knopf, 1975).
15.   'Oh you beautiful monster', interview with Jack Pierce, *New York Times*, 29 January 1939.
16.   'Whale and Frankenstein'.
17.   Clarke interview with Mank.
18.   Ibid.
19.   Ken Beale, *Boris Karloff, Master of Horror* (New Jersey: Gothic Publishing, 1966).
20.   'Whale and Frankenstein'.
21.   Mike Parry and Harry Nadler, *Castle of Frankenstein*, 9, 1966.
22.   Ibid.
23.   Marilyn Wood, interview with Gregory Mank, Los Angeles, 1992; quoted in *Films in Review*, 1990.
24.   Ibid.
25.   Art Ronnie, 'Frankenstein Revisited', *Southland Sunday*, December 1971.
26.   Interview with Colin Clive, *New York Times*, quoted in *Frankenstein* script book.
27.   'Whale and Frankenstein'.
28.   Clarke interview with Mank.
29.   Dennis Gifford, *Karloff the Man, the Monster, the Movies* (New York: Curtis Publishing, 1973).-

Chapter seven

AN early preview of *Frankenstein* left the specially invited audience in shock. The Laemmles, particularly Junior, were extremely anxious, unsure whether Whale's film was terrifying, morbid or even blasphemous. They confessed to the *Motion Picture Herald* that 'they did not know what to do about it'. Eventually, cuts were ordered. Gone was Colin Clive's 'Now I know what it feels like to be God!' – the cut covered by a peal of thunder – gone were three close-ups of Fritz torturing the Monster and, most importantly, the contentious drowning of little Maria was excised, despite Whale's determination to keep it in. The *Motion Picture Herald* opined: 'I won't forgive Junior Laemmle or James Whale for permitting the Monster to drown a little girl before my very eyes'. Instead, the sequence cut away at the point where the Monster reaches for Maria, leaving the rest to the audience's imagination. Karloff was pleased, Whale was philosophical.

After the hysterical reaction to the first preview, a special opening was shot, featuring Edward Van Sloan directly addressing the audience, which must have tickled Whale's bizarre sense of humour:

> How do you do? Mr Carl Laemmle feels that it would be a little unkind to present this picture without just a word of friendly warning. We are about to unfold the story of 'Frankenstein'. A man of science, who sought to create a man after his own image, without reckoning upon God. It is one of the strangest tales ever told. It deals with the two great mysteries of Creation: Life and Death.

I think it will thrill you. It may shock you. It might even *horrify* you. So, if you feel that you do not care to subject your nerves to such a strain, now's your chance to – Well ... we warned you ...

Universal arranged a West Coast preview of *Frankenstein* in Santa Barbara, and Whale drove up with David Lewis late in November 1931. As before, the audience were absolutely terrified: people fainted or walked out, and one mother and daughter fled the cinema and ran screaming into the street.

Whale and Lewis spent the night of the preview at the Biltmore Hotel, Santa Barbara, no doubt anxious as to the fate of the film. Whale fell into a deep sleep, but was woken at around three in the morning by the phone ringing. He picked up the receiver:

'Are you the man who directed the movie they showed tonight?' said a voice.

'Yes,' said Whale.

'Well, I can't sleep and I'll be goddamned if I'm going to let *you* sleep!'

With such a reaction, Whale must have sensed *Frankenstein* was something special, but no one could have been prepared for the sensational business the film did upon its release in December 1931, taking $53,000 in its first week. An opening day advert in the *New York Daily News* on 4 December declared: 'A creature – half man, half fiend – a soulless wretch with a mechanical brain – knowing every human sensation except the love of a woman. To see it is a badge of courage! No-one [was] seated during the final reel!' The Laemmles were delighted, particularly as the adverse publicity they had feared merely strengthened the film's box-office appeal. 'I never intended this picture for children,' smirked Whale, 'but would like to make a children's version.'[1]

Boris Karloff, who was not invited to a single preview, eventually saw the whole film during Christmas 1931. During a visit to an old schoolfriend in San Francisco, he and his wife Dorothy headed across the bay to Oakland to check out the new sensation:

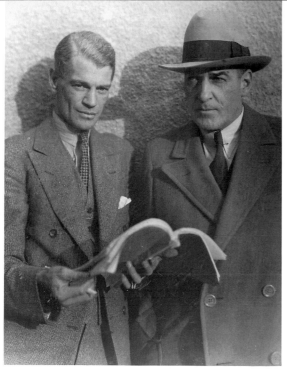

Whale and mob-exposing author Dean Sullivan outside Tiffany Studios, 1930. Courtesy of Ronald V. Boorst/ Hollywood Movie Posters.

Dwight Frye as Fritz in *Frankenstein* (1931). Author's collection.

Universal Studios roll-call, 1932. Whale is back row, eighth from left. Fourth from left, Boris Karloff; tenth from left, Bela Lugosi; twelfth from left, Raymond Massey. Front row centre, Carl Laemmle, Sr. Courtesy of Ronald V. Borst/Hollywood Movie Posters.

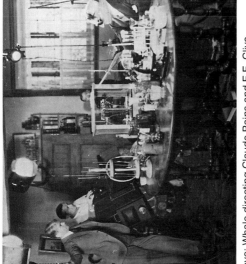

above: Whale directing Claude Rains and E.E. Clive on the set of *The Invisible Man* (1933). Arthur Edeson is behind the camera. Courtesy of Ronald V. Boorst/Hollywood Movie Posters.

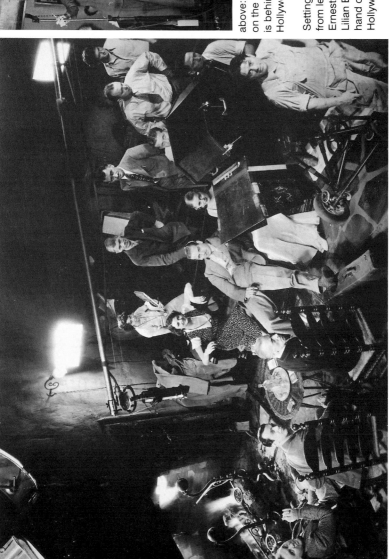

Setting up a shot on *The Old Dark House*. Seated from left, Charles Laughton, Raymond Massey, Ernest Thesiger, Gloria Stuart, Melvyn Douglas, Lilian Bond. Whale is behind Douglas with hand on hip. Courtesy of Ronald V. Boorst/Hollywood Movie Posters.

Whale studies the script of *The Bride of Frankenstein* (1935). Courtesy of Ronald V. Boorst/ Hollywood Movie Posters.

The morning after the night before. Edward Arnold interrogates his suspects in front of Charles D. Hall's beautiful deco sets in *Remember Last Night?* (1935). Robert Young is by the fireplace, Constance Cummings seated. Author's collection.

Whale and Paul Robeson on the
set of *Showboat* (1936).
Author's collection.

Three comrades. Maurice Murphy,
John King and Noah Beery Jr
in *The Road Back* (1937).
Author's collection.

865

Whale's impressive riot scene for which a special camera crane was built in
The Road Back (1937). Author's collection.

A rare candid shot of Whale and his dog outside his beloved studio, *c.* 1950.
Author's collection.

Whale in Paris, 1951. Author's collection.

below: One of the last pictures of Whale, sitting near the pool, c. 1956. Author's collection.

The pool, built on land next to Whale's studio in the early fifties. Author's collection.

72

Whale and Karloff play up for the press on the set of *The Bride of Frankenstein*. Courtesy of Ronald V. Boorst, Hollywood Movie Posters.

Tiffany Studio portrait of Whale, 1929. Author's collection.

What could be more natural than to invite our friend to a performance? I had, of course, seen rushes of the picture, but never a connected version, and as the film progressed, I was amazed at the hold it was taking upon the audience. At the same time I couldn't help wondering how my own performance would weather all the build-up. I was soon to know.

Suddenly, out of the eerie darkness and gloom, there swept on the screen, about eight sizes larger than life itself, the chilling, horrendous figure of me as the Monster!

And, just as suddenly, there crashed out over the general stillness the stage whisper of my wife's friend. Covering her eyes, gripping my wife by the shoulder, she screamed:

'Dot, how can you live with that *creature*?'[2]

The film made a star of Karloff, but the reviews were fulsome in their praise for Whale too. In press interviews, he adjusted his age from forty-two to thirty-five and spoke of having had private tutors in his youth in England. The transformation was complete. Whale had created his new self just as efficiently as Frankenstein created his monster.

The film ran into a few more problems with the censor, including an unbelievably dim request from the state of Massachusetts: 'Eliminate scene showing body on slab coming to life.'[3]

After the incredible success of *Frankenstein*, all concerned began to look around for another project. Universal didn't seem to know what to do with Karloff, and wasted him in such cheapies as *The Cohens and Kellys in Hollywood* and *Night World* with Mae Clarke and Lew Ayres. Whale, basking in the glory of *Frankenstein*'s reception, cooed: 'I'm getting quite to like Hollywood. It makes me so brown and beautiful'.[4]

Whale was next asked by Laemmle to take charge of a modest little film called *Impatient Maiden*. The screenplay, based on Donald Henderson Clarke's book *The Impatient Virgin*, was by *Frankenstein* collaborator Francis Edward Faragoh and not up to much. Whale was keen to flex his new-found cinematic skill, however, and, after the original director Cyril Gardner was removed from the project, he took control. Whale clearly had little interest in it as it wasn't in any sense a personal project, but he asked for Mae Clarke to feature and was given Lew Ayres as his star. The story was a silly one, concerning ambulance man Ayres's infatuation for the dizzy Clarke: 'She couldn't wait for life to unfold its secrets. She was determined to dig them out for herself. My! How her eyes were opened when she met the real man.'

Lew Ayres recalled that Whale gave him no direction whatsoever, merely bouncing his crossed leg in his familiar fashion. This was to become a familiar pattern in Whale's career. He would throw himself body and soul into pet projects, but simply bring others in on time and within budget. It is sometimes possible to notice how much care he lavishes on the scenes which interest him, and how little he bothers with the more mundane. This is particularly true in *Frankenstein*, where the romantic interludes between Mae Clarke and John Boles contrast sharply with the more macabre elements. David Thompson, in *A Biographical Dictionary of the Cinema*, commented: 'It is all too clear that some sequences engrossed him, while on others he didn't give a damn.'[5]

After finishing – and forgetting – *Impatient Maiden* (audiences and critics did the same), Whale returned briefly to England for his first visit since *Frankenstein*'s triumph. Back in Hollywood, Junior Laemmle was keen to rush a sequel to *Frankenstein* into production, and poor Robert Florey submitted another outline, 'The New Adventures of Frankenstein – The Monster Lives!' His idea was given short shrift, but he was told to prepare *The Invisible Man* and *The Wolf Man* for Karloff, who had by now signed a star contract with Universal. Florey, already wary of the Laemmles, insisted upon a proper, cast-iron contract, but this was deemed impossible and he was taken off both projects.

Thus, Whale found himself inheriting from Florey again and, in January 1932, he prepared a treatment for a version of *The Invisible Man*. This, the only extant work by Whale, was declared unacceptable, possibly by Whale himself who never considered himself a writer (see Appendix A). In addition, Whale was reluctant to do another horror film. It would be ironic if he had escaped the pigeon-hole of 'war director' only to find himself classified as a 'horror director'. Laemmle, though, pressed for Whale to find a suitably scary vehicle for his new star, 'Karloff the Uncanny'. Remembering an obscure J B Priestley novel which had amused him, he asked Laemmle to snap up the rights. The book, *Benighted*, concerned a group of travellers trapped overnight in a bizarre Welsh household. In America it had been published as *The Old Dark House*, and that was the title it retained when Whale asked his old friend Benn Levy to adapt the book for the screen.

The novel was intended by Priestley as quite a serious piece of social criticism masked under the guise of a conventional horror story. The protagonist Roger Penderel is a cynical war veteran, who feels rejected by the society he risked his life to save. The bluff Yorkshire millionaire Sir William Porterhouse represents the grasping, class-conscious *nouveaux riches*, and the family Femm, owners of the titular house, all the vices and obsessions of Edwardian England, which Priestley saw as clinging so tenaciously to the present day. Typically, none of this really interested Whale. What he saw was a bizarre and blackly comic story which would provide an ideal vehicle for his talents. Laemmle was pleased because the film provided a role for Karloff (albeit small) as the brutal, mute butler Morgan. With all sides content, Whale set to work casting the film which, perhaps above all his others, can be regarded as the work of an *auteur*.

Whale assembled a wonderful cast. Ernest Thesiger was brought over from England especially to play the skeletal Horace Femm. Eva Moore, then mother-in-law of Laurence Olivier, became the deaf religious maniac Rebecca Femm, Melvyn Douglas took the part of Penderel, Raymond Massey and Gloria Stuart featured as the bickering Philip and Margaret Waverton and Brember Wills, another special English import, played the mad brother Saul. Perhaps the most pleasing casting for Whale was to employ Charles Laughton as Sir William Porterhouse. Having played Laughton's own son only four years before, it must have been satisfying for Whale to give the great stage actor his first screen experience.

Laughton was in Hollywood to film *The Devil and the Deep* for Paramount, but the script wasn't quite ready so Whale grabbed him for *The Old Dark House*. Elsa Lanchester was very pleased to see Whale again, though Laughton kept his customary distance from the 'showy' director. Despite this, the Laughtons invited Whale to dinner several times during their stay, along with other ex-pats Thesiger and Lilian Bond, who joined the cast as Sir William's chorus-girl fiancée. On the Laughtons' first night in the then smog-free California, Whale took them to the famous Brown Derby restaurant for dinner: 'Jimmy Whale said, "You will love it here in Hollywood, Charles. I'm pouring the gold through my hair and enjoying every minute of it!" Charles was horrified by that. But Jimmy did love money.'[6]

Having already worked with Raymond Massey (in *Prisoners of War*) and the immortal Ernest Thesiger, whose camp archness appealed greatly to Whale's sense of humour, it was a very happy set. Whale had seen Gloria Stuart playing in *Peer Gynt* and *Romeo and Juliet* at the Pasadena Playhouse. She was then under contract to Warner Bros., but Whale was sufficiently impressed to ask for her to be loaned out to Universal. Stuart would make a further two pictures for Whale and remembered *The Old Dark House* with great affection:

> I was very snobbish about film. I really was headed for the New York Theatre. But I thought it would be easier to go as a movie actress than cold, but I was wrong. Working with James Whale taught me a lesson. He was a man of enormous taste. He had been an actor so he was very helpful in interpreting a role. He was precise, calm and, once in a while, very sarcastic! But mostly very pleasant and *very* much in charge.[7]

Stuart admitted to finding Whale initially intimidating, but soon warmed to him and the two became friends:

> My initial impression of James was that he was very austere, very cold, very English – very removed from the scene! He was not at all 'cozy' or anything. ... With James, every single line, every single movement, your whole approach to the character was very meticulously discussed. He was the most prepared director I ever worked for. ... He had every scene

mapped out before-hand. I remember seeing his script and he had all the camera moves on the blank, left-hand side of the page.[8]

Whale knew just what he wanted to achieve with the film. Although intended, and marketed, as a horror film, he could get away with a great deal of his own very particular humour within the context of the picture. For it to work on both levels, however, he would have to keep a tight rein on his cast:

> All the actors in *The Old Dark House* were very sophisticated, knowledgeable and experienced, and Whale ran a very tight ship. Karloff was very quiet – after all, he had been under all the heavy makeup beginning at four in the morning – but he was beautifully educated, very soft-spoken and charming. Laughton was there, with his 'method'; he had to huff and puff in a scene, so he ran up and down the stage to huff and puff, which was an eye-opener for me – I can huff and puff without moving a muscle!
>
> All the actors – Raymond Massey, Melvyn Douglas, all of them – they were stage-trained, very fine, accomplished actors, they all rehearsed a great deal until James had everything exactly the way he wanted it.[9]

On the evidence of *The Old Dark House*, Whale was obviously having a ball. Benn Levy's screenplay stripped down the Priestley novel to its bare essentials, retaining much of the witty dialogue and substituting shocks for social comment. The result is a flamboyant, hilarious and absolutely bizarre film.

Whale opens with three travellers, Philip and Margaret Waverton and their mysterious friend Roger Penderel, as they struggle through a hellish storm somewhere in Wales. Penderel is Whale's outsider for this film, indifferent to where he is going or how he will get there. A mud slide forces the travellers to seek refuge in the Femm's house, where the front door is opened by mad butler Morgan (revealed only as a single, burning eye, rather than with the familiar three close-ups). Waverton attempts to explain their predicament, but Morgan merely grunts unintelligibly and slams the door. 'Even Welsh ought not to sound like that!' twinkles Penderel.

Whale is clearly in his element here, neatly balancing traditional scares with black humour.

It is the appearance of Horace Femm, though, which really sets the tone of the film. Embodying everything which his effete name suggests, Ernest Thesiger as the dried-up, atheistical Horace is all veiled threats and sinister quips. 'My sister was on the point of arranging these flowers,' he says, before throwing them into the fire. Later he informs his guests, 'We make our own electric light here.' The lights fade and die. 'But we're not very good at it.'

As the Wavertons continue to argue and we are introduced to Horace's deaf sister Rebecca – 'No beds! They can't have beds!' – we discover more about Penderel's enigmatic personality. Horace offers gin and a toast to illusion. He then enquires if Penderel is one of the young men who have been 'knocked about a bit by the war'. Penderel's reply could almost have come from Whale himself: 'War generation, slightly soiled. A study in the bittersweet, the man with the twisted smile.' Whale gives him a tiny moment of reflection and then undercuts it with 'And this, Mr Femm, is excellent gin,' hurriedly masking this tiny slip in his assumed front of cynical indifference. Penderel seems to be Whale's voice throughout, detached and amused by the proceedings despite everyone else's terror.

Margaret Waverton is escorted to a bedroom by the fearsome Rebecca Femm to change out of her rain-drenched clothes. Miss Femm fondles the beautiful dress: 'That's fine stuff – but it'll rot.' She extends a hand towards Margaret's bosom: 'That's finer stuff still – but it'll rot too, in time!' Rebecca Femm proceeds to explain the house's wicked past and how her sister Rachel, her spine injured in a fall from a horse, had lain in the bedroom screaming until she died. How her sinful, lusty brothers and her father Sir Roderick (102 and still alive – upstairs) filled the house with wicked women. Whale brilliantly distorts the old hag's face in the mirror, affording each line a different, increasingly bizarre cut: 'You're wicked too! You think of nothing but your long straight legs and your white body, and how to please your man!' Whale then slyly has Miss Femm vainly checking her hair in the mirror as she departs.

The Old Dark House is full of such touches. Charles D Hall's shadow-wreathed set is as lopsided and crazy as the family Femm themselves. Gloria Stuart remembered the subsequent scene, in which she flees down a storm-swept corridor from the brutal Morgan's lusty gaze and her vision of Rebecca Femm's reflected warnings:

> I said to James, 'I don't understand it – everybody else is in rain-drenched clothes, and here I am, changing, in a pale pink, bias-cut evening dress with the avanti straps.' I said, 'I don't get it, James.' And he said, 'As you run, and later, when Karloff chases you, I want you to go through the walls like a flame.'[10]

Whale shifts between grotesque humour and genuine alarm. The brutal Morgan, keeper to the family's maddest member Saul, is given a variation on the traditional sequence of three close-ups. As he claws lecherously at Margaret Waverton, we see first his eyes, then his broken nose, and finally his salivating mouth, until Philip Waverton knocks him unconscious with a lamp. With Morgan out of action, the Wavertons explore the upper levels of the house and, passing the locked door where Saul is kept, discover the bedridden Sir Roderick. In a high, cracked voice, the ancient invalid warns them that his entire family is insane and that Saul – a pyromaniac – is the worst of them all. This is frightening information, both for the Wavertons and the audience, but Whale is having fun all the time. He cast a *woman*, Elspeth Dudgeon, as Sir Roderick, gave her a wispy beard and billed her in the credits as *John* Dudgeon!

For the final section of the picture, Whale almost reverts to the stark mood of *Frankenstein*. Having lulled his audience into a false sense of security with his black humour, he delivers one shock after another. Drunk and vindictive, Morgan releases Saul, whom we first see as a clawed hand on the bannister. After the tremendous build-up, Saul is revealed as a rather sad little man, who protests that his family keep him locked up because he knows they actually killed his sister Rachel. Whale then brilliantly cuts back to Saul's benevolent expression which, once unobserved, turns immediately into one of blatant madness. This is a genuinely scary moment, and Whale doesn't let up now until the end of the film.

Penderel is locked in a battle of nerves with the knife-wielding Saul and then a vicious fight, which takes them both crashing through the balcony to the floor. In Priestley's novel both men die, but Whale, perhaps remembering his comments on *Frankenstein*, opts for a happy ending, giving Lilian Bond a nice in-joke as she tends to the injured Melvyn Douglas. 'He's alive!' she shrieks, *à la* Colin Clive. 'Alive!' A final, poignant scene arrives as Morgan finds his beloved Saul dead and cradles him in his arms, weeping bitterly. This is a heart-breaking moment, beautifully played by Karloff, who shows an extraordinary, almost homoerotic grief at the death of his charge.

Whale switches back to the film's familiar style for the end, a traditional, sunny 'morning after' with Thesiger waving his unwanted guests goodbye with a Queen Mary-esque – 'So nice to have met you!' – and Melvyn Douglas, rescued from his cynicism by his love for Lilian Bond, proposing marriage as Charles Laughton snores contentedly nearby.

The finished film is a delight, in which Whale is able to take great liberties without risking the integrity of the piece. As Gregory Mank observed in *American Cinematographer*:

> *The Old Dark House* is unique amidst Whale's famous, oft-seen horror shows: it survives, almost bitterly, almost defiantly, as the director's most unusual work, a terror tale showcasing his own style, with the least incense-burning to public taste. Stocked with horror flourishes, it is primarily a high exercise in macabre comedy, peopled with ensemble eccentrics, playing on a mad level above the head of many audiences, perhaps delighting the vision of the director more than any audience member who paid to see the new Karloff show in 1932. While Karloff's Morgan is legendary, the role is small; there are no historic special effects; the star, really and truly, is the director.[11]

During production of the film, Whale had written to R C Sherriff, inviting him to come out and write screenplays for Erich Maria Remarque's sequel to *All Quiet on the Western Front*, the grim and prophetic *The Road Back* and H G Wells's *The Invisible Man*.

Sherriff and his mother came west and visited the set of *The Old Dark House*. Sherriff even contributed bits of dialogue to Levy's script and participated in the same tea-time ritual which had occurred on *Frankenstein*. For Gloria Stuart, this was the only sour note in the production:

> With the exception of Melvyn Douglas, the whole cast was English and they were very much apart. They had elevenses and fourses – tea at eleven and four – and Melvyn and I were never asked to join. There was no social conversation. At least not with me.[12]

If the English kept themselves apart from Douglas and Stuart, it did not extend to life outside the studio. Whale took to Stuart and, together with David Lewis, was her escort on several occasions:

> James took me to the theatre many times – Jane Cowl, Katherine Cornell, all the greats that came to Los Angeles – and he was a wonderful companion. Off the set, he had a very sharp sense of humour, and he could be very cutting, too – he really could cut you off at the pass! Away from the set, he was charming and relaxed, but back on the set next morning, it was 'Ach-tung' time.[13]

As the picture neared completion, Whale took Sherriff to see the Laemmles to talk about *The Invisible Man*. After the usual platitudes as to his fine writing credentials and affirmations that 'Jimmy Whale reckons you're the man to do it', Sherriff was given an office on the Universal lot and a pile of the unworkable screenplays which had already been commissioned. He was dismayed by the absurd lengths to which other writers had gone to 'improve' on Wells's story. One screenplay switched the action to Tsarist Russia, another made the protagonist into an alien who threatened to flood the world with invisible Martians!

Sherriff reasoned that the best approach was to return to the book he had loved so much as a child and, after a long search of the Los Angeles bookshops (Universal had lost their only copy!) he came across the novel. His problem now was that he was expected to write the screenplay in his noisy office on the Universal lot. Whale, who by now understood the workings of the Laemmle mind, sympathized. Over lunch at the Universal commissary he told Sherriff: 'All we want is a good job, and you can't do that unless you go about it in your own way. It's one of the rules of the studio that everybody on the payroll comes in at the proper time in the morning.'[14]

Whale advised Sherriff not to be an odd-man out, but to turn up with everyone else, give his secretary something to type and then spend some time looking round the studio:

> There's plenty to see. Come in and watch me shooting *The Old Dark House* and pack up after lunch. You see the point? If you're in at the right time in the morning that's all that matters. There are people going out all day on various business, and you go with them. Spend the afternoons as you want to, and get to work in the evenings in your room at the Chateau Elysee in the way you've been used to at home.[15]

This pleased Sherriff, and he set to work. In the meantime, Whale finished work on *The Old Dark House* and was asked by Junior Laemmle to direct a curious little melodrama which the studio had developed from a play by Ladislaus Fodor. Whale was anxious to begin work on *The Invisible Man* but Sherriff's screenplay wasn't ready so, as ever keen to keep working, he prepared *The Kiss Before the Mirror*.

It was a complex and interesting story, pleasingly dark, concerning an attorney brought in to defend an old friend against a charge of murdering his unfaithful wife. After listening closely to his friend's account of the deterioration of his relationship, the attorney begins to see the same signs in his seemingly idyllic marriage. Junior Laemmle wanted Charles Laughton for the part of the attorney and Whale too was keen, but Laughton returned to England for what was to become his Oscar-winning triumph in Korda's *Private Life of Henry VIII* (1933). Instead Whale signed Frank Morgan as the attorney and Nancy Carroll as his faithless wife. *The Kiss Before the Mirror* is a delicate and unusual film bolstered by excellent performances, particularly Paul Lukas as the defendant.

The film opens like a light operetta as Lukas's wife (Gloria Stuart) strolls through a twilit garden to meet her lover (Walter Pidgeon), who proceeds literally to waltz her through the house. The atmosphere is romantic almost to the point of saccharine, but Whale knows what he is doing. Out of nowhere, a window shatters and a bullet kills Stuart. The guilt-stricken Lukas explains himself to Morgan in a series of beautifully photographed vignettes: the two men alone in pools of light inside a claustrophobic darkness. Karl Freund, who had just made his directorial debut with *The Mummy*, replaced the unavailable Arthur Edeson on camera, and did a fine job.

The film climaxes with an impassioned speech by Morgan which secures Lukas's release, leaving Nancy Carroll in no doubt that unless she ends her own affair she will suffer the same fate as Gloria Stuart.

Filmed in a highly theatrical style (Whale cheerfully carries his camera through several artificial walls), *The Kiss Before the Mirror* is pitched in near-operatic mode as a highly stylized piece of cinema. It was well received at the time, and Whale was particularly pleased with the results. Loyal as ever to those he liked, Whale reused both Gloria Stuart and Paul Lukas, as well as Freund and Ted Kent, who became film editor for most of the rest of Whale's pictures.

By now, Sherriff's screenplay for *The Invisible Man* was complete, and Whale drove down to Santa Monica to congratulate the writer. Having sat up reading it most of the night, Whale was absolutely delighted. Its simplicity, particularly important because of the special effects which could so easily swamp the story, appealed to him and the characters were delightfully eccentric:

> It knocked all those other adaptations into a cocked hat. They couldn't hold a candle to it . . . Whale was an old friend. We understood each other so well that it had been in my mind to confide in him that everything I had written was pure and simple Wells, Wells from start to finish: that all I had done was to dramatise and condense the story to fit the screen. But on second thoughts I decided to keep quiet about it. The script had put me so high in his estimation that there

wasn't any point in watering it down. He had obviously forgotten the original novel: all that concerned him was that I'd produced a work of genius, and he was the happier because I had been his protégé.[16]

Whale was being pushed to make a sequel to *Frankenstein*, but the idea did not appeal to him and he thought the existing script quite dreadful. The clarity and excellence of *The Invisible Man* script would give him ample reason to wriggle out of the sequel, so long as he could persuade Junior of its merits. 'I'm not just using your script as a way of getting out of this horrible *Frankenstein* sequel,' he told Sherriff. 'It's a lovely job, and I'd do it if I had a hundred scripts to choose from.'[17] Whale cleverly contrived to make the script appear 'hot' by virtually demanding that Junior take an evening off to read it:

> Take the script home and don't look at it till you've had your supper. Then tell them you're not to be disturbed for the rest of the evening. I needn't tell you not to go to bed till you've finished it, because once you begin reading it nothing on God's earth will make you put it down till you've finished it.[18]

By this time Junior Laemmle was so impressed that he forgot all the bombastic superlatives he was accustomed to and enquired, 'You mean it's good, Jimmy?'

The next day, the studio was buzzing with the news of the brilliant new script for the long-delayed Wells film. Junior Laemmle's only concern, apart from the special effects, was that his star, Boris Karloff, had walked out on Universal after a protracted wage dispute. In truth, the studio was in dire financial trouble, but Karloff's departure pleased Whale immeasurably. He had his own plans for the leading part of Griffin 'the Invisible One': in short, his old friend from the distant days of *The Insect Play*, former RADA lecturer Claude Rains. Laemmle, however, balked at this. Rains was unknown in America and, despite his beautiful voice (all that would register of him until the final frames of the picture) it would be suicidal to risk him in such a high-profile and costly venture. Rains had made a test for RKO's *A Bill of Divorcement*, a disastrous experience which the actor recalled with great amusement: 'Along came a test of a man called Claude Rains. Well, they howled with delight! But Whale said "I don't give a hang what he looks like. That's how I want him to sound and I want HIM!"'[19]

Whale was determined to get his way, but in the meantime tried to placate Laemmle by suggesting Colin Clive. This was an acceptable choice, but Whale was able to convince his old friend that Rains was the only man for the job and Clive declined, returning to England. Whale made a final push for Rains by arguing that the film would be a sensation because of its effects, not because of its star. Finally, after much anxiety, Junior Laemmle caved in.

Rains was signed, as were Gloria Stuart and William Harrigan, replacing Universal contract player Chester Morris who walked out after refusing to share top-billing with newcomer Rains. In addition Whale brought in two players whom he liked immensely and who would contribute their particular brand of Englishness to his later pictures: the shrieking Una O'Connor as Mrs Hall, the publican's wife and E E Clive as the walrus-moustached P C Jaffers, who would memorably remark upon first 'seeing' the invisible Rains, "E's all eaten away!'

Delighted with his cast and Sherriff's excellent script (H G Wells voiced his disapproval of Sherriff's device of a dangerous drug affecting his hero's sanity, but Whale laughed it off, reasoning that only a lunatic would want to be invisible in the first place) Whale turned his attention to the technical problems of successfully achieving the invisibility effects.

Certain scenes were possible using wires, but Universal's head of effects, John P Fulton, had to work long hard hours with Whale to perfect some of the more complicated effects. Rains was clothed from head to toe in black velvet with his costume over the top, and shot against an identical backdrop. Using double-exposure techniques, Rains was then fitted into the live action, his clothes realistically filled, but his head and hands invisible. However, an unexpected complication arose, much to Whale's annoyance, and he shot off a memo to Martin Murphy[20]:

From James Whale   April 1, 1933
Subject 'REDLIGHT SIGNALS'

Time and again the perfect take has been ruined by motor
cars and trucks driving past the red light signal outside the
Invisible Man stage. If a general warning does no good I
think a watchman would save the company at least twelve
times his salary.

James Whale

Murphy immediately ordered all concerned to 'stop and kill their
motors while the red light is on, and not to proceed until after it has
been flashed off'. Whale was sufficiently respected to get an instant
response to his requests.

Claude Rains remained very patient as Whale ploughed
through the complications of the special effects. Gloria Stuart,
however, found Rains's unbending professionalism and seriousness
a little hard to take:

> It was Claude's first film and he and James worked very
> closely together on what was, for most of the time, a closed
> set. It was a very pleasant experience but I wasn't too crazy
> about Claude. Actors, I find, have enormous egos, much
> more so than actresses and Claude was fine, most of the time.
> Every once in a while, though, he would try and back me out
> of the shot and James would say, 'Now Claude, be *nice* to
> Gloria,' and we'd do the scene over.[21]

The Invisible Man opens in true Whale style with an
introduction in darkness, and what an atmospheric introduction it
is. Griffin staggers through the snow towards The Lion's Head, an
authentically English pub full of beer-swilling villagers, telling tall
tales and playing darts. Suddenly, the door is flung open and Griffin
is framed in the doorway. The characteristic three short close-ups
reveal a bandaged face, a suspiciously artificial-looking nose and
dark goggles. He cuts a swathe through the frightened clientele and
demands a room.

Whale builds the suspense as the mysterious stranger is
shown to his room by the landlady (Mrs Hall) and gazes out onto the

snow-bound landscape. He has some luggage at the station. Can it not be fetched tonight? Is there a key to the door? The stranger wants to be left alone. A little unnerved, Mrs Hall brings him his supper but forgets the mustard and returns, unannounced. In a truly startling shot, we see Griffin eating, the whole bottom half of his face missing! Griffin, it transpires, has turned himself invisible with a rare and dangerous drug. While he searches for an antidote, he little realizes that the drug turns anyone who takes it quite mad ...

Back at Griffin's laboratory, his sweetheart Flora and her father Dr Cranley wonder where the young scientist has 'disappeared' to. Flora is distraught and as unresponsive to the wooing of Griffin's rival Dr Kemp as was Mae Clarke to John Boles's approaches in the similar triangle in *Frankenstein*.

Frustrated by his failure to find an antidote, Griffin turns violent, attacking the hysterical Mrs Hall and her husband. The police are called and Griffin relishes the chance to show the world his transformation. Whale presents a genuinely chilling shot of Griffin unbandaging his head, and for a moment – sans wig, nose and goggles – he resembles a grinning, mummified skull, cackling insanely:

Man: Go on, arrest him!

Jaffers: How can I handcuff a bloomin' shirt?

Griffin escapes and, invisible, enters the home of his rival in love Dr Kemp, to whom he explains his insane plans: 'We'll start with a few murders. Great men. Small men. Just to show we're not choosy.'

Jack Griffin is a variation on Henry Frankenstein: a driven and dedicated scientist forced into a quest of knowledge by his ambition. Although Whale clearly empathizes with his outsider, there is little evidence of the compassion afforded Frankenstein or his monster. In fact, for all its ghoulish humour, *The Invisible Man* is a quite shockingly nasty film. A bicycle is ridden down a village street, apparently by no one, but a woman's pram, complete with baby is knocked over. A pair of trousers skip hilariously down a country lane as their invisible occupier sings, 'Here we go gathering nuts in May', but later he batters a policeman to death with a stool.

This juxtaposition of black comedy with quite shocking violence seems to have particularly appealed to Whale, whose sense of humour undoubtedly exhibited a vicious streak from time to time.

Only once does Whale allow Griffin a moment of compassion. Flora comes to see him before the police close in and, for a moment, we glimpse the old Griffin, the dedicated scientist unaware of the dangers of his vital work. Soon, though, the drug reasserts its influence and Griffin crows insanely: 'Even the moon is frightened of me. Frightened to death!'

He embarks on a reign of terror but is eventually caught and shot, betrayed by the footprints he leaves in the snow. Griffin dies in a hospital bed, Flora at his side, returning slowly to visibility as his life ebbs away, and affording us our first glimpse of Claude Rains in the entire film.

The Invisible Man remains one of Whale's finest achievements, an absolutely dazzling thriller with brittle humour and still impressive effects. R C Sherriff, back home in England, was delighted: 'It was the first talkie to let itself go on trick photography, and Whale had handled the story beautifully.'[22]

As a result of the film's spectacular success, Sherriff was offered *The Four Feathers* by Alexander Korda and began a lucrative and prestigious career in British films. Claude Rains became a star overnight, just as Karloff had been before him. H G Wells, his disquiet about the invisible drug notwithstanding, was delighted with the film, particularly Una O'Connor's portrayal of the shrieking Mrs Hall. For Whale, it was a source of great pleasure to have scored a hit when Universal needed one so badly.

Notes

1.   'James Whale and Frankenstein', interview, *New York Times*, 20 December 1931.
2.   Peter Haining (ed.), *The Hollywood Nightmare* (New York: Taplinger Publishing, 1971).
3.   David J Skal, *The Monster Show* (London: Plexus Publishing, 1994).
4.   Gregory William Mank, *The Hollywood Cauldron* (Jefferson, NC: Macfarlane, 1994).

5. David Thompson, *A Biographical Dictionary of Cinema* (London, 1980).

6. Elsa Lanchester, *Elsa Lanchester Herself* (London: Michael Joseph, 1983).

7. Gloria Stuart, interview with the author, Los Angeles, May 1994.

8. Ibid.

9. Gloria Stuart, interview with Gregory Mank, Los Angeles, 1988; quoted in *American Cinematographer*, October 1988.

10. Ibid.

11. Gregory Mank, quoted in *American Cinematographer*, 1988.

12. Stuart, interview with the author.

13. Stuart interview with Mank.

14. R C Sherriff, *No Leading Lady* (London: Victor Gollancz, 1968), p. 257.

15. Ibid.

16. Ibid., p. 268.

17. Ibid., p. 269.

18. Ibid., p. 270.

19. Claude Rains, *Universal Weekly*, 1933.

20. Whale, memo to Martin Murphy, University of Southern California Archive.

21. Stuart interview with the author.

22. Sherriff, *No Leading Lady*, p. 287.

Chapter eight

BY the beginning of 1934, Whale's relationship with David Lewis had sufficiently developed for them to consider buying a house together. They chose a beautiful, white single-storey property in Pacific *Palisades*, close to the ocean, at 788 South Amalfi Drive and moved in together. This was highly unusual, even in the atmosphere of Hollywood, where the movie colony's bohemianism was, to a certain extent, tolerated. However, Whale and Lewis's relationship must have aroused some degree of gossip. David Chierichetti, biographer of bisexual director Mitchell Leisen, describes the atmosphere of the times:

> Hollywood at that time was such a small town. It was divorced from everything – even from Los Angeles. In the days before the Hays Code began to bite, there was a feeling that movie people were wild and strange.
>
> I don't know of any other case like Whale and Lewis. It was very unusual. Men lived together – as confirmed batchelors – but even that was difficult. Cary Grant and Randolph Scott lived together for some time until Paramount, to whom they were under contract, put an end to it. I mean, they were both married to women who were never there! But certainly with Whale and Lewis it must have been frowned upon. Hollywood's attitude was that anybody could do it as long as they were discreet, as long as they covered their tracks. Mitchell Leisen's secretary told me that David Lewis was a 'pansy' and it surprised me that she was so blunt and pejorative about it, because she was a lesbian! But she said he was a 'pansy' because he was *so* open about it. [1]

It is interesting to speculate whether Whale's undeserved reputation as 'The Queen of Hollywood' stems from his relationship with the more flamboyant Lewis. Was he, in fact, found 'guilty by association'?

Lewis was at that time working with Merian C Cooper at RKO, but would shortly resign and be taken on by the legendary Irving Thalberg at MGM under whose tutelage he advanced quickly. Whale, who was able to pay for the entire house, effectively kept Lewis during this lean period for the young man. Whale plainly didn't give a damn what people thought, and, despite this reserve and discretion, may have caused trouble for himself by living so openly with Lewis. David Chierichetti again:

> Gay people today make such an effort to have associations and so forth, but in the 'Thirties it was kind of the opposite. If a person were suspected of being homosexual, the worst thing they could do would be to hang out with other gay people – unless they were a costume designer, in which case it was accepted. All the Hollywood costume designers seemed to be gay.
>
> The studios were like families. Paramount in particular. Everyone was very close. I don't think there would have been any effort at that time for gay people to get together and talk about mutual concerns. I think even when they ran into each other they tended to be more careful, even though they *knew*.
>
> Directors like George Cukor always met up with people like Cole Porter and tried to get them into his films. Irving Thalberg had some 'tendencies' and employed a lot of gay people – like David Lewis – but whether or not there was a kind of 'secret movie society', I really don't know.[2]

Whatever reputation his relationship with Lewis was garnering him, Whale was still under contract to Universal and protected by his excellent working relationship with Junior Laemmle. As long as he continued to turn out hits like *Frankenstein* and *The Invisible Man*, Laemmle would allow him total creative freedom. Whale had little reason to care what the rest of Hollywood thought of him.

Before the move to Amalfi Drive, Whale had begun planning an adaptation of John Galsworthy's *Over the River* – the last of the Forsyte novels. In addition, he was hard at work on an original screenplay for Boris Karloff entitled *A Trip to Mars*, which he hoped R C Sherriff would write for him. Sherriff was already preparing *The Road Back*, but Laemmle was unhappy with the script and the project was effectively in limbo.

In mid September 1933, however, Junior asked Whale to replace Robert Wyler as director on *By Candlelight*, a slender farce based on a popular German play. The story concerns a butler (Paul Lukas) who is mistaken for his aristocratic employer (Nils Asther) by the maid (Elissa Landi) of a countess. The butler, in turn, mistakes the maid for her employer and the two fall in love. An amusing, if slight, picture it benefits from some lovely performances and lustrous photography. Unusually for Whale, the score is dominant and *almost* becomes tiresome, so that virtually the whole film plays like the opening scenes of *The Kiss Before the Mirror*.

Whale brought his new editor Ted Kent on board, but made few other alterations to Robert Wyler's team. He was pleased to work with his friend Paul Lukas again and finished the film in October of that year.

As the end of 1933 approached, Whale began preparation on the Galsworthy project, to be known by its American title, *One More River*. Tired, however, after the exertions of *The Invisible Man* and *By Candlelight*, he decided to take a holiday in England. Ostensibly, he would be working with Sherriff on *One More River*, but it would be enjoyable to see the old country again and he intended to visit his family. The local paper in Dudley ran the following excited report:

Mr Whale Returns

One of Dudley's famous sons is expected home for a holiday this Christmas. This is Mr James Whale, the film producer, who made his name with *Frankenstein* and *The Old Dark House*, and is now one of Hollywood's most highly-paid directors. A graduate of the Birmingham Repertory Theatre,

Mr Whale made several stage appearances before he took to producing. One of his earliest successes was *Journey's End*. I am told that Mr and Mrs Whale who live in Park Hill Street, Dudley and are both 78 years of age, have not seen their brilliant son for over a year, so that this Christmas re-union will be a great occasion for them.[3]

Whale's three nieces (the daughters of his brother Arthur) maintained that Whale was so against any fuss upon his return home that he once declined the Freedom of Dudley. Nevertheless, it must have been gratifying for him to return to his humble origins in such splendour, bestowing fabulous Christmas presents on his appreciative relatives. The nieces were always thrilled to see him, and remembered his humour and powers of mimicry: 'A visit from Uncles James was a continual round of splendid diversion. Humorous, intellectual, enlightening and revealing. Never, never boring.'[4]

Whale returned to London, where he visited Sherriff to discuss *A Trip to Mars* and had pictures and designs made for *One More River*.

When he finally came back to Hollywood, refreshed and keen to work, Laemmle told him that *A Trip to Mars* was to be dropped, and pressed once again for Whale to work on 'The Return of Frankenstein'. Whale was still opposed to the sequel so, in order to get the project up and running, Laemmle gave it to director Kurt Neumann. In the meantime, Whale moved into the house on Amalfi Drive and began pre-production on *One More River*.

Galsworthy's novel was chiefly concerned with the doomed relationship of society débutante Dinny Charwell, but a secondary plot strand told of the messy divorce of Dinny's sister Clare from her brutal husband Sir Gerald Corven. Sherriff thought Galsworthy's attempts to highlight the ludicrous English divorce laws made for the more interesting part of the novel and, after extensive consultation with Whale, concentrated on the lesser theme for his screenplay.

Whale was very pleased with the script and was determined to be as true as possible to the novel's Englishness – no easy task in

Hollywood. With this in mind he assembled a sturdy British cast headed by the wonderful Diana Wynyard as Lady Clare and the British colony's elder statesman in Hollywood C Aubrey Smith as her father. Colin Clive was back again, this time as the villainous Sir Gerald, and the immortal Mrs Patrick Campbell turned in one of her rare film performances as Wynyard's aunt. In supporting roles he gave Jane Wyatt her break in the now much-reduced role of Dinny Charwell; Lionel Atwill a splendid cameo as the prosecuting counsel and *The Invisible Man*'s E E Clive a very amusing role as a seedy private detective.

It is *One More River*'s exquisite detail which marks it out as distinctive. William K Everson called it 'By far Hollywood's most successful attempt at putting *any* aspect of England on the screen.'[5]

Whale opens the film with Lady Clare's return from Ceylon. She and the charming young man, Tony Croom, who has fallen in love with her during the crossing, are saying their goodbyes. Whale presents us with vivid and shaded characterizations. Clare is capable of flirting with the impressionable Tony despite, or perhaps because of, her recent split from her husband, who has assaulted her with a riding crop. Sir Gerald, another study in tortured darkness from Colin Clive, genuinely loves his wife but wants to control her. In order to get his way he alleges adultery between Clare and Tony, a charge which, to save her name, the lady must fight.

Whale treats the main drama very seriously and with great intensity, though he enjoys himself immensely with his minor characters: E E Clive's adoption of a variety of ludicrous disguises to eavesdrop on the alleged lovers; and a seemingly psychic hat-check man who never forgets which hat belongs to who (his secret revealed only when Whale shows us the little notes he keeps pinned inside the brims).

In particular, though, Whale evidently loved working with Mrs Patrick Campbell, the glorious old trout who has all the film's best lines. As Jane Wyatt attempts to explain the intricacies of her sister's unhappy marriage, Mrs Pat wonders about the virtues of reincarnation, deciding that she would like to come back as a goat: 'A he-goat, for preference,' she decrees, 'so as not to be milked.' Later, as she retires to bed followed by her real-life companion, her dog Moonbeam, she complains of pains in her side. 'I don't know whether it's flatulence or the hand of God!' she trills.

There is an embarrassment of English detail: the ancient couple who haven't voted for anyone since Gladstone are authentic, and not merely an American idea of cheerful English eccentrics; and the local pub, The Blue Pig, looks right even if the name is a joke. Only the lush Californian sunshine seems wrong: even the best of English summers never seem to have light so pure and dazzling. Most intriguingly, perhaps, is the sureness of foot Whale displays in his handling of the British aristocracy. It is as though he had been around these people all his life, an impression which would undoubtedly have pleased him. His ease in dealing with a level of society for which he had no natural affinity is extraordinary, and he seems as much at home with an ancient English family like the Charwells as with any of the colourful working-class grotesques of his other films.

Colin Clive is given the standard entrance. Referred to before he arrives, he moves from deepest shadow into dazzling light and is afforded the familiar three jarring close-ups. He is a villain, but, in keeping with the flavour of the film, a restrained and well-bred one. In fact, the whole film is remarkable for its sensitivity and naturalism. Clive Denton concluded that the film, 'draws from Whale a more direct and concerned response to everyday human feelings than is usual in his work'.[6]

One More River climaxes with a brilliant courtroom sequence in which Whale's camera is never still, roaming around a room designed to appear almost unnaturally tall with artificially high doors and bookshelves. William K Everson wrote in *Films in Review* that the bravura editing and drama of the climax make it 'quite possibly the best courtroom sequence ever filmed'. Lady Clare loses the case and her honour, but is free of her dreadful husband and can now admit to herself just how she might feel about the devoted Tony Croom.

Whale removed a scene in which Clive effectively rapes his estranged wife, and the incident (save for a brief flashback) is only indirectly referred to in the finished film, lending it far more poignancy and menace as a result. *One More River* is a real gem and it remains a great shame that it is virtually forgotten today. William K Everson concluded:

> the exactitude of all the detail might well not be apparent to US audiences, but it doesn't matter – the 'rightness' of everything would still get through, if only subliminally . . . the film works on so many levels – as film, as a Whale film, as translated Galsworthy, as social comment – that it could be used beneficially by any class using film.

At the end of shooting, Whale asked Colin Clive to stay on in Hollywood as he had another project in development. The *Frankenstein* sequel had not progressed under Kurt Neumann, and Whale finally gave in to Junior Laemmle's pleading. On another critical high from *One More River*, Whale planted his tongue firmly in his cheek and began preparation on what was to become *Bride of Frankenstein*.

If Whale had to make a sequel, he insisted it would be entirely on his own terms. From its inception, the film was intended as a pitch-black comedy. He told Sherriff that he considered he had milked the original idea dry, therefore the only solution was to take an entirely different approach. Rather than the stark realism of the original, Whale wanted a fantasy of epic proportions and a great deal more of the macabre humour in which he so liked to indulge.

Like *The Invisible Man*, the screenplay had already been through numerous treatments. An early example, by L G Blechman, made Henry and Elizabeth Frankenstein into carnival puppeteers, escaping their past. The Monster finds them and demands a mate, which Frankenstein supplies via a high-tension wire hooked up to a carnival wagon. The experiment is doomed, of course, and the Monster is savaged to death by an escaped lion! After Philip MacDonald's very modern version (concerning Henry Frankenstein's attempts to sell a death-ray to the League of Nations) was rejected, John L Balderston came up with an unsettling screenplay rather reminiscent of his original in tone. In it, the female Monster is pieced together from the carnage of a train crash and has the 'head and shoulders of a hydrocephalic circus giantess who has committed suicide in a fit of sexual despondency'.[7]

Balderstone's work was completely at odds with the director's vision of the film, so he brought in writer William Hurlbut to produce something more to his taste. A draft was sent to the much-despised Joseph Breen at the Production Code Administration, who was responsible for passing all Hollywood's scripts before filming. By 1934, censorship was beginning to bite and Breen objected strongly to the script's religious references and generally irreverent tone. Whale corresponded with Breen, and a letter dated 10 December 1934 survives, showing Whale to be firmly in cheeky mood:

> Dear Mr Breen,
>
> Herewith are the proposed changes, which deal with your letter of Dec 5, and also your letter of December 7. As, however, the former letter is fuller, I think it best to send on the letter I had written immediately after the conference, as in your letter of December 5 there are several points about God, entrails, immortality and mermaids which you did not bring up again, and I am very anxious to have the script meet with your approval in every detail before shooting it.
>
> All best wishes,
>   Yours sincerely,
>   James Whale[8]

What Whale eventually got away with was far too subtle to be noticed by Mr Breen and his fellow censors. Interestingly, the finished screenplay returned to Mary Shelley's original novel for several episodes, most famously his meeting with a blind hermit in the woods.

Whale's problem would be to satisfy those eager for genuine horror, while at the same time getting away with as much tongue-in-cheek campery as he could. He confessed to David Lewis that he was approaching the whole endeavour as a 'hoot' but, even though he was now secure as Universal's 'Ace' director, he would have to walk a very narrow margin between comedy and terror in order not to alienate both his audience and Junior Laemmle. Karloff recalled how they resolved one particular problem:

The producers realized they'd made a dreadful mistake. They let the Monster die in the burning mill. In one brief script conference, however, they brought him back alive. Actually, it seems he had only fallen through the flaming floor into the millpond beneath, and could now go on for reels and reels![9]

Karloff was happy to reprise the role which had made him a star, and Whale assembled a magnificent supporting cast even before the screenplay was finished. Una O'Connor and E E Clive returned from *The Invisible Man* and Whale specially imported the Australian actor O P Heggie for the role of the saintly blind man. Mae Clarke was no longer available for Elizabeth so the part went to a seventeen-year-old English actress Valerie Hobson. She remembered that Whale first introduced her to Colin Clive in their bedroom scene:

> The first time I ever saw Colin Clive, I was dressed in a flimsy nightgown, and had to climb into bed with him. And I was introduced to him as I arrived in the bed! Jimmy Whale: 'Mr Clive, this is Miss Hobson. Now let's get on with the scene!' So James Whale must have had a sense of humour, because that was a bit far-fetched even for Hollywood![10]

The part Whale clearly enjoyed most was created especially for his dear friend Ernest Thesiger – the wispy, arch Dr Septimus Pretorius, apparently Frankenstein's old tutor until he was 'booted – no less – out of the University, booted my dear Baron, is the word, for knowing too much'. Pretorius is Thesiger's finest hour, even outdoing his Horace Femm of a few years previously. It is a delightful performance: camp, shrill, frightening and oozing malevolent bitterness from every pore. On the set, Thesiger would indulge in his needlepoint (he was an acknowledged expert) and discuss ideas with Whale for the look of the Monster's mate. Together they created a bizarre Nefertiti-like image for the female creation – but who would play her? Whale, ever loyal to his old friends, knew at once: Elsa Lanchester, now well-established after her triumph as Anne of Cleves opposite her husband in *The Private*

Life of Henry VIII, was the perfect choice. What really tickled Whale was to cast her in two roles, as both the female Monster and Mary Shelley herself in the film's delicate prologue:

> I do have an odd face, and James was absolutely dead set that my face was the face for the Bride of Frankenstein!
>
> James's feeling was that very sweet, very pretty people, both men and women, had very wicked thoughts inside ... evil thoughts. These thoughts could be dragons, they could be monsters, they could be of Frankenstein's laboratory. So James wanted the same actress for both parts to show that the Bride of Frankenstein did, after all, come out of sweet Mary Shelley's soul.[11]

The gentlemanly Karloff, as ever, suffered for the part, but only clashed with Whale over one aspect of the screenplay: giving the Monster the power of speech, which he considered a stupid mistake: 'My argument was that if the Monster had any impact or charm, it was because he was inarticulate ... this great, lumbering inarticulate creature ...'[12] Whale disagreed. For him, the notion of the Monster being educated, taught to drink and even smoke, was part of the fun. It was up to Karloff to convey this with all the skill he could muster. He managed it beautifully, creating a sepulchral voice which is at once heart-rending and lifeless.

Whale seems to have slightly resented Karloff's success, having been responsible, as it were, for the star's 'creation'. Relations had been fairly cordial on the first picture, but Whale bristled at Karloff's new-found status – the former extra was now billed above everyone, including Colin Clive. When the press came on set, Whale went out of his way to poke fun at Karloff, even posing with the stand-in dummy of the Monster as though to imply that the actor contributed the same impact to the picture. Elsa Lanchester remembered this well:

> That was a thing in which James Whale was rather nasty. He was very derogatory about Boris Karloff; he'd say, 'Oh, he was a *truck* driver.' Maybe, in the early days, he had to do some hard work, but Boris Karloff was a well-educated, very gentle, very nice man.[13]

Whale's construction of his aristocratic persona had been so successful that he almost seemed to believe his own propaganda. Karloff was, in fact, the theatre-loving black sheep of a family of British diplomats, precisely the kind of family from which the working-class Whale so wanted to have sprung.

When *Frankenstein* was first released, it had been previewed before two Catholic priests in order to gauge how offensive the film's themes would prove to the important Canadian market. Although they found nothing wrong with the film they recommended that the censors could be placated by the addition of 'a suitable foreword or some preface that would indicate the picture was a dream. Perhaps we could open on the book with the off-scene voices of Shelley and Byron discussing a fantastic tale and dissolve into the picture'.[14] Whether or not Whale ever knew about these plans for his original, it was exactly the method he decided upon to open the sequel. He felt at liberty to start completely afresh by presenting the story as springing directly from Mary Shelley's lips, thus giving him more licence to experiment with the film's form.

The film opens on a stormy night in Switzerland as the camera moves into the more appealing interior of the house in which the Shelleys and their infamous friend Lord Byron are living. Young Mary is afraid of the lightning, which Byron finds astounding: 'Look at her, Shelley, can you believe that bland and lovely brow conceived a Frankenstein – a monster created from cadavers out of rifled graves. Isn't it astonishing?' Mary laughs this off. After all, the three of them are scarcely paragons of virtue.

> Mary: ... I say look at Shelley – who would suspect that pink and white innocence, gentle as a dove, was thrown out of Oxford University as a menace to morality, had run away from his lawful spouse with innocent me but seventeen ... reviled by society as a monster himself. I am already ostracized as a free thinker, so why shouldn't I write of monsters?

Whale knew he was playing with fire in this sequence, but he wanted to establish the right mood for the film and clearly had a great deal of affinity with Mrs Shelley's sentiments.

Byron reminisces about the original story and we are treated to a montage of shots from *Frankenstein*, beginning with the never-used tableau of the mourners against the sky and ending with the Monster's apparent death in the blazing mill. This isn't the end of Mary Shelley's story, however, and Whale fades from the Lake Geneva setting to the skeletal remains of the mill ...

Gloating over the Monster's demise is Una O'Connor as Minnie, housekeeper at Castle Frankenstein. She is 'dour and cadaverous' according to the script, 'her aged emotions ... fed and glutted on violence, obscenity and death'. There is a burst of flame from the blackened timbers, much to the terror of a villager, Marta:

Marta: Isn't he dead yet?

Minnie: That's his insides caught at last – insides is always the last to be consumed.

Minnie is clearly an extension of O'Connor's portrayal of Mrs Hall in *The Invisible Man*, and Whale clearly adores using her ghoulish character, even though Joseph Breen got his way and changed 'entrails' to 'insides'!

Whale then counterpoints this black humour with the grief of Hans and his wife, parents of little Maria, drowned by the Monster in the first film. Hans won't be satisfied until he has seen the Monster's 'blackened bones', but he ventures too close to the ruins of the mill and falls into the flooded cellar beneath. In a truly startling shot, Whale then shows us the Monster, burned and scarred by the fire, emerging from behind a beam to drown Hans. The Monster climbs from the cellar, extending his hand to Hans's wife. She takes hold of it, but realizes too late that it is not her husband and the Monster dashes her down to her death in the cellar. Immediately after this, Minnie stumbles upon the Monster and, hitching up her skirt, flees towards the village. The Monster's reaction? A tiny and hilarious double take. Within a very few minutes, Whale has established the tone of the picture: humour juxtaposed with horror at every turn.

It transpires that Henry Frankenstein is not dead, much to his fiancée's relief, but determined to put the dark days of his experiments behind him. He will have no more of 'the dust of the dead'. Until, that is, the sinister Dr Pretorius arrives on a matter of 'grave importance'. Pretorius sweeps in – 'a very queer-looking gentleman', as Minnie puts it – and insists on seeing Frankenstein alone. Elizabeth is dismissed from her intended's bedroom by Pretorius who, like a desiccated homosexual imp, tempts Henry away from all that is safe and natural.

Back in his own lodgings, Pretorius proposes a toast to his hoped-for collaboration with Frankenstein: 'Do you like gin? It's my only weakness. ... To a new world of Gods and Monsters!' With these words, Whale treats us to an in-joke for those who enjoyed *The Old Dark House* (the gin), a sly reference to Pretorius's sexuality (his *only* weakness?) and a credo for living which could have come directly from Whale's lips, and which is extended further slightly later in the film:

> Pretorius: Sometimes I wonder if life would not be much more amusing if we were all devils, and no nonsense about angels and being good.

Finally, Pretorius reveals the fruits of his own labour, which he has *grown* from cultures: 'My experiments did not turn out *quite* like yours, Henry – but Science, like Love, has her little surprises, as you shall see.'

Bizarrely, Pretorius has created seven tiny people whom he keeps in jars. The first is a queen, in full costume; the second, 'quite naturally', a king (modelled slyly on Charles Laughton's Henry VIII); the third a disapproving bishop; the fourth the Devil himself with ' a certain likeness to me – don't you think? Or do I flatter myself? I took a *great* deal of pains with *him*.' These are followed by a ballerina (beautiful but boring, as she won't dance to anything but Mendelssohn's Spring Song), a mermaid (an experiment with seaweed) and finally a baby pulling a flower to pieces which, the script comments, looks as though it 'might develop into Boris Karloff':

> Pretorius: I think this baby will grow into something worth watching.

The entire sequence is a joy, not only for Whale's clever in-jokes, but in the way he still manages to maintain a sinister veneer to the proceedings via Thesiger's waspish malevolence. The tiny creatures are funny but rather disturbing. As Frankenstein comments, it is more like black magic than science. Undeterred, Pretorius has an idea:

> Pretorius: Leave the charnel house and follow the lead of Nature ... or of God – if you like your Bible stories – 'male *and* female created He them. ... Be fruitful and multiply'. ... Create a race ... a man-made race upon the face of the Earth. ... Why not?

Mary Shelley's original novel has long been seen as a proto-feminist work, voicing quite natural fears about the progress of science in the hands of men, and how those same men would eventually seek a means of procreation which didn't involve women at all. The blatantly homosexual Septimus Pretorius seems to exemplify the theory, indeed the novelization of *Bride of Frankenstein* by Michael Harrison (writing as Michael Egremont) makes the point even more baldly:

> Pretorius: Come, 'be fruitful and multiply'. Let us obey the biblical injunction: you, of course, have the choice of natural means; but as for me, I am afraid there is no course open to me but the scientific way.

Whale had been criticized by Joseph Breen for the irreverent attitude to religion taken by the screenplay (Pretorius's 'if you like your Bible stories' was originally 'if you are fond of your fairy-tales'), but the censor apparently failed to notice Whale's blatant allusion to the Monster as *Christ* throughout the film. After a chase through Whale's expressionistic forest, the Monster is finally captured by the mob. Brutalized, beaten, misunderstood and unwanted, the tragic creature is 'raised against the sky, a terrible but pathetic sight – friendless, persecuted and almost crucified. The baying of the hounds and the murmurs of the mob – some savage, some jubilant, only accentuate the dumb appeal on the Monster's face.' The Monster is actually trussed up on a cruciform pole, then thrown down into a cart and transported to prison.

Whale, while perhaps not an atheist, had very little time for organized religion, and took the opportunity here to subversively mock Christianity through Pretorius's quips and the Monster's treatment at the hands of the villagers. He always maintained sympathy for the Monster – his ultimate outsider – and enjoyed slipping such blasphemies past the Breen office. In the sequence with the blind man, which follows the Monster's escape from prison, Whale shows the Monster weeping as the hermit thanks God for alleviating his loneliness: 'Ave Maria' swells on the soundtrack and a crucifix on the wall retains a glowing after-image as the scene fades. What Joseph Breen may have taken as a belated measure of respect is actually the opposite: Whale gently mocks the blind man and his religion for discovering the answer to his prayers in the shape of a seven-foot tall, murdering monster.

The Monster is happy with his new friend – indeed, as two of society's outcasts, the two men form a perfect combination. The hermit teaches the Monster to speak, drink wine and smoke cigars, and it is a measure of Karloff's sincerity that this potentially ludicrous situation is so sympathetically presented. Of course, this idyll cannot last. Society intrudes in the form of two hunters who recognize the Monster for what he is and, unthinkingly, 'rescue' the blind man from the only friend he has.

Alienated from a world he has tried to embrace, the Monster seeks solace in the only company he knows – the dead. Toppling a graveyard statue (the original script has him attempting to rescue the figure of Christ from a similar structure), he finds his way into a crypt, which is in the process of being robbed by none other than Dr Pretorius. Their plans are perfectly linked: Pretorius, cackling madly as he eats his supper off a coffin, is in search of the bones he will need for the female creation; the Monster wants a mate:

> Pretorius: I think you can be very useful – And you will add a little force to the argument if necessary. Do you know who Henry Frankenstein is – and who you are?
>
> Monster: Yes – I know – He made me from the dead – I love the dead – Hate the living.

Pretorius wins the Monster's confidence and forces the unwilling Frankenstein to collaborate with him by kidnapping Elizabeth. In the truly electrifying creation sequence, Whale used 175 different shots, many uplit at bizarre angles, to convince the audience that 'a miracle is about to take place'. The new creation comes alive and is revealed in all her glory as Pretorius announces 'The Bride of Frankenstein!', Franz Waxman's magnificent score cheekily echoing the theme of the wedding march.

The Monster is naturally delighted, but it soon becomes apparent that all is not well. 'Friend?' appeals the Monster. His bride screams. The ideal heterosexual union which Whale has been parodying ends in failure: the Bride hates her mate just as much as the rest of society. There can be no victory for the Monster even when he attempts to mimic those who despise him.

Elizabeth has managed to escape and bursts in to rescue Henry. The Monster, his arm poised on the lever which will blow up the laboratory, allows them to go, for they must live. Pretorius, however, is less fortunate. The Monster recognizes him for the arch-manipulator he is, a kindred spirit who is separate from society. The malevolent, Godless, amoral Professor must remain behind:

Monster: You – stay. We belong dead!

Henry and Elizabeth escape, the Bride gives a truly frightening final hiss and the Monster pulls down the lever, blowing the laboratory to pieces.

Bride of Frankenstein is quite rightly considered the high point of the 1930s horror cycle, and possibly the best film of its kind ever made. Gregory Mank, writing in his production background to the published screenplay of the film, concluded:

it is certainly Whale's masterpiece, a three-ring Swiftian circus of sardonic wit, theatrical flourishes of terror, and bitter morality. Whale did more than conjure up the Romantic theory which Mary Shelley had evoked: that there can be no sympathy in our prearranged universe for a being created by man and not God. With elegant audacity, Whale went Mrs Shelley one better and made Karloff's Monster a bizarre Christ symbol, who laughs and weeps and pleads with those great, scarred hands with an almost heart-breaking humanity.[15]

Notes

1. David Chierichetti, interview with the author, Los Angeles, May 1994.
2. Ibid.
3. 'Memories of Dudley'; quoted in *Memories of Dudley* (Dudley, Worcs: Beacon Broadcasting, 1989).
4. 'Master of Horror', *Black Country Bugle*, April 1981.
5. William K Everson, *Films in Review*, 1962.
6. Clive Denton, *James Whale: Ace Director* (New York: C. Denton, 1979).
7. David J Skal, *The Monster Show* (London: Plexus Publishing, 1994).
8. Ibid.
9. Arlene and Howard Eisenberg, 'Memoirs of a monster', *Saturday Evening Post*, 3 November 1968.
10. Valerie Hobson, interview with Gregory Mank; quoted in *Bride of Frankenstein* script book (New Jersey: Magic Image Film Books, 1989).
11. Elsa Lanchester, interview with Gregory Mank, Los Angeles, 1979; quoted in *Bride of Frankenstein* script book.
12. Mike Parry and Harry Nadler, *Castle of Frankenstein*, 9, 1966.
13. Lanchester interview with Mank.
14. Skal, *Monster show*.
15. Gregory Mank, quoted in *Frankenstein* script book.

Chapter nine

Bride of Frankenstein completed shooting ten days late and $100,000 over budget, but Whale was delighted with it. There was some dispute with Junior Laemmle over the amount of humour in the film when the public was expecting undiluted horror, but the film was released nonetheless. The *Hollywood Reporter* enthused:

> one of the finest productions that has come off the Universal lot for many a day. Mounted extravagantly, gorgeously photographed, excellently cast. Karloff is superb as the Monster . . . Elsa Lanchester, in a dual role . . . is excellent . . . beautifully acted and directed.

After the initial previews, however, the studio decided to cut the film by some fifteen minutes. The opening Shelley sequence was cut drastically, removing all references to the three sinners' moral behaviour; an entire sub-plot involving Dwight Frye as an avaricious peasant who uses the Monster to murder his relatives was excised; and the seventh of Dr Pretorius's homunculi – the Karloff-like baby played by midget Billy Barty – was also removed. Whale thought his film benefited from a shorter running time, but he did request that Boris Karloff return to shoot a single scene to replace the missing material, in which he encounters a band of gypsies and burns his hand in their fire.

With all concerned finally happy, the film was put on general release and immediately did excellent business, playing an incredible eleven times a day at the 2,812-seat Pantages Theatre. Whale was at the top of his form, in complete control of virtually every aspect of his films. His latest hit was, in a complete sense, 'A James Whale Production'.

Bride of Frankenstein was the first of seven pictures personally produced by Junior Laemmle in 1935. He had stepped down from his position as head of production to concentrate on projects close to his heart, though rumours were sweeping Hollywood that Universal was in very serious financial trouble. The success of *Bride* helped the situation somewhat, but plans for Whale to begin work on *Showboat* were nevertheless stalled due to its million-dollar budget. A large proportion of Universal money was at that time being pumped into John Stahl's *Magnificent Obsession* (1935), which was to prove one of the costliest films then made.

While waiting for the go-ahead on *Showboat*, Whale came up with another project, this time based on a novel he had read called *The Hangover Murders*. What he finally produced, as lustrously photographed as *Bride* and, in many ways, a companion piece to it, is nothing less than a lost screwball classic: a murder mystery with a streak of pitch-black, cynical humour.

Whale assembled a memorable cast, including Robert Young and Constance Cummings (by then married to Benn Levy after a failed romance to Junior Laemmle) as newlyweds Tony and Carlotta Milburn; Edward Arnold as the hard-boiled detective Danny Harrison; Edward Brophy (whose murderous hands were grafted onto Colin Clive in Karl Freund's *Mad Love* that same year) as his dim-witted assistant Maxie; and the wonderful Arthur Treacher as the po-faced butler Phelps:

> Tony: Pardon me, Phelps. Is that a cocktail or a nervous affliction?
>
> Phelps: It's a side-car, sir.
>
> Carlotta: Well, open it up and we'll all jump in.
>
> Phelps: A *dozen* glasses?
>
> Tony: Mrs Milburn is feeling playful.
>
> Phelps: *Yeees*, sir.

The story concerns a group of rich drunks who spend a delirious night on the town and awaken next morning to find one of their number, Vic Huling, murdered. The trouble is, they were so drunk that any one of them could have killed him.

At Junior Laemmle's request, Whale changed the title to the ironic *Remember Last Night?* and constructed the whole film with a sureness and lightness of touch which is frequently dazzling. He turns the whole thriller convention and the world on its head (even opening with a traditional 'end of film' kiss between Robert Young and Constance Cummings) by never letting seriousness intrude for more than a few brief moments. Even the mounting body-count is rarely allowed to interrupt the terrific, high-speed wisecracking:

Maxie: What did you find out?

Harrison: Shot through the arm, the bullet travelling transversely to the heart where it stopped.

Maxie: The bullet or the heart?

Harrison: *Both*.

Maxie: Suicide, huh?

Harrison: Yeah, he shot himself through the heart, then got up and hid the gun.

Maxie: I see. So it's *moider*!

Harrison: Remarkable. Coroner, meet Dr Watson.

Coroner: Delighted, Doctor. Medical or Ph.D.?

Maxie: Ah, go count the shingles on the roof.

Whale's camera is amazingly mobile, moving effortlessly through several walls and up a staircase in one, fluid movement. There is one particularly delirious montage sequence, complete with multi-lens shots of champagne bottles, as the revellers indulge in their trawl; a bizarre and rather scary blackface dance sequence; and a scene in which the Milburns take pot-shots at a nearby yacht with a cannon!:

Bette: What was that?

Penny: The marines have landed.

Bette: There'll be atrocities – I want to be first!

The yacht proceeds to beat a speeded-up retreat which is straight out of a cartoon.

The film is full of Whale's little touches. The party-goers' bitchy comments are frequently accompanied by the offscreen wailing of cats. Robert Young strolls around in his wife's fluffy negligée, much to the consternation of the police. 'Just a little thing I picked up in Poret's,' camps Young. 'Don't let it upset you.' Even the redoubtable E E Clive shows up as the Coroner's photographer, advising that 'it would make a better composition if you would move the head of the corpse just a little further to the right.'

Whale was very fond of *Remember Last Night?* and the excellent ensemble playing of his cast, but the film's amoral tone somewhat baffled critics and it was never the success it deserved to be. Constance Cummings remembered Whale, and the experience, with affection: 'He was a most delightful man. Urbane, gentle and very warm, with a nice off-beat sense of humour.'

By November 1935, Whale was finally allowed to start work on *Showboat*, which would be the last film under his original Universal contract. The story of the Mississippi river-boat and its extended family had already been filmed once by Laemmle Snr in 1928, but sound was in its infancy then and Universal was convinced that a lavish new version would set the box-office alight. Whale was deemed an unusual choice for the director of such a piece of Americana, but Junior Laemmle had every confidence in him. Whale told the *New York Post* that, 'as an outsider I had a better appreciation of the situation, and, because I realized how much I really don't know about the Mississippi, I surrounded myself with people who knew everything'.

His cast included the excellent Irene Dunne as Magnolia, Charles Winninger as Captain Andy, Allan Jones as the gambler Gaylord Ravenall and, most memorably, Paul Robeson and Hattie McDaniel. The tragically shortlived Helen Morgan completed the main cast as Julie. To design the costumes, Whale turned to his former fiancée Doris Zinkeisen (by then one of London's foremost designers), who obliged with 300 stunning watercolours which Universal made up with great fidelity.

Whale was determined to prove his versatility. *Showboat* gave him an extremely rare chance to bring his cinematic gifts to a subject radically different to his usual material. Although sensible enough to bring in help when out of his depth (LeRoy Prinz was commandeered from Paramount to supervise the dance sequences), Whale was completely at home with the compellingly human drama that unfolds on board the ship. He wanted the action to be far more naturalistic than is usual in a musical, and his *Showboat* is one of the few filmed musicals to have background action continuing during a song – as it does, of course, in life.

There was a little friction on the set over Whale's headstrong determination to do it his way. He told the cast that he didn't care how they might have done it before, this would be *his* interpretation. Allan Jones took an instant dislike to Whale and remained dismissive of his direction for the rest of his life:

> None of us were very happy with Jimmy Whale. It would have been a much better picture with a different director. He was a very strange man. Stand-offish. I never knew what the hell he was thinking.
>
> It needed to be warmer. The cutting wasn't tight enough. He needed to bring in the numbers a little smoother. He'd never done a musical. Just all those *Frankenstein*'s, *All Quiet on the Western Front* or whatever the hell he did.[1]

Irene Dunne, too, thought he was wrong for the film, but her relations with Whale on set were far more cordial. During the blackface number 'Gallavantin' Around' – which surprised and delighted audiences used to a rather more genteel Miss Dunne – she rose to the challenge: ' "Whatever is true to the part and good for the picture is OK with me," was her comment, to which the delighted James Whale added: "Spoken like a lady, an artiste and a trouper!" '[2] During the show within the show, in which members of the company act out a Victorian melodrama, Whale was heard to shout, 'Make it worse! Make it worse!'

David Chierichetti, who knew Irene Dunne well in her last years, recalled her feelings about the film:

> Universal was such a strange studio. The Laemmles were on their way out, partly because of the cost of *Magnificent*

Obsession, and they had Irene Dunne under contract for two films. They'd decided to remake *Showboat* but they so seldom did any films like it that they didn't really have a musicals production group like MGM and Warners.

Irene did think Whale was a bad choice and that he really didn't direct her *at all*. This is probably true but he didn't need to. I wonder to what extent anybody directed her. She was a very strong performer although not the kind of actress who would get into fights with her directors. I think she basically did on film what she had done on stage and it worked out very well. She always considered *Showboat* one of her favourite films.[3]

Showboat is perhaps most notable for its treatment of the black characters. Again, Whale strongly identified with society's outsiders, giving them a realism and warmth which is highly unusual in a Hollywood picture of the 1930s. During Dunne's blackface routine, Whale cuts from the gaiety of the theatre to a shot of the blacks-only section of the auditorium, as if to emphasize the isolation of an entire race by their white masters. Likewise, the scene in which Julie (of black birth but fair enough to pass for white) is banished from the showboat is beautifully realized and very poignant.

Whale became great friends with Hattie McDaniel and Paul Robeson, even contemplating a further movie, *Black Majesty*, with Robeson which, sadly, came to nothing. *Showboat*'s highlight, however, is Robeson's most famous number, the immortal 'Ol' Man River'. Like *Frankenstein*, it has been so often imitated and parodied that it is easy to forget the original impact of this wonderful song. Whale was obviously aware of its significance and lavished great care on its realization. Robeson recorded the song only two feet away from the microphone, lending it a quiet dignity which the more usual booming interpretations lack. On set, Whale surrounded Robeson with elaborate, expressionistic montages of black slaves labouring under cotton sacks and hurled into dingy jails, moving in an extraordinary 270-degree pan as the song reaches its climax. It is an intensely moving moment. Black historian Donald Bogle wrote: 'Robeson never fully demeaned himself, and when he sang "Ol' Man

River" . . . he lifted the entire movie onto his massive shoulders and carried it to moments of eloquence and greatness.'[4]

Whale shot far more footage than he ever intended to use and, eventually, was left with an amazing 300,000 feet of exposed film. *Showboat* was released in April 1936 with incredible success, as the reviews testified. *Variety* was fulsome in its praise:

> When James Whale was first suggested as the director it was doubted if an Englishman was the best choice for a subject so thoroughly American. Result looks as if Whale had been born on the Mississippi. His sensitive guidance of the players is mainly responsible for the excellence of the production.

The *New York World-Telegram* was equally complimentary:

> Universal has done right by our great American classic – *Showboat*. It moves across the screen – a grand pageant of song, sentiment and loamy nationalism. . . . James Whale has done a beautiful job of direction and the cast responds to him with a perfection that at times is astonishing, notably in Paul Robeson's superb singing of 'Ol' Man River'.

Whale was absolutely delighted. He had completed his Universal contract with a smash hit and was free to look around for new projects.

Universal itself, however, had finally succumbed to the financial problems which had plagued it almost from birth, and control of the studio passed out of the Laemmle's hands to a new consortium headed by J Cheever Cowdin and Charles R Rogers. At the time, Whale didn't fully appreciate the significance of this event. He was glad to be free of his contract, rewarding though it had been, and welcomed the chance to explore new horizons. He travelled to London for the opening of *Showboat* and began negotiations with Junior Laemmle concerning the independent production company which Junior wanted to set up. Laemmle told the press: 'I have made arrangements to form a company which will produce four big pictures a year for a major distributing corporation which I am not at liberty to name.' Shortly afterwards, he officially contracted Whale and scenario-writer Jerry Horwin.

Whale himself gave a rare interview to the *New York Post* on the back of *Showboat*'s huge success: 'That they should pay such high salaries is beyond ordinary reasoning! Who's worth it? But why not take it? And the architecture! And the furnishings! I can have modernistic designs one day and an antiquated home over night! All the world's made of plaster of Paris!'

Meanwhile, David Lewis had talked Irving Thalberg at MGM into making James Hilton's *Goodbye, Mr Chips* in England. R C Sherriff had written the script, and Whale was set to direct with Charles Laughton starring. It was to be Lewis's first credit as solo producer and, potentially, the start of a whole new chapter in Whale's film-making career. MGM, unlike the troubled Universal, was a major-league studio, and after a string of box-office smashes, crowned by the success of *Showboat*, it was only natural that Whale should move on to greater and more prestigious work.

Whale was very fond of *Goodbye, Mr Chips* as a novel and, unsure how he stood with the new regime at Universal, relished the chance of making the movie for MGM. What was even better than the very British subject matter was the chance to make *Chips* in England. The irony would not have been lost on Whale that, as a British director, he had never made a film in his native land. As a bonus it would be good to spend more than a few fleeting weeks in the old country.

Lewis arranged for Whale to meet Irving Thalberg, and the two men got on very well. Thalberg offered Whale $75,000 a picture, which was fine, but wanted no time limit on the production, which wasn't. Through Lewis, Whale knew how much Thalberg liked to interfere and that production of a movie could drag on and on until he was satisfied. For Whale, it was important to make a movie as quickly and efficiently as possible, then move on to something else. His experience on *Hell's Angels* had taught him the agonies of extended production. Unfortunately, just as these problems were being ironed out, Charles Rogers called Thalberg and pleaded with him not to take Whale on. Universal, he stressed, had only two top directors, Whale and John Stahl. If the 'New

Universal' were to be successful, they had to keep all the talent they had. Reluctantly, Thalberg gave in.

Goodbye, Mr Chips was finally made, splendidly, under the direction of Sam Wood and starred Robert Donat and Greer Garson. Whale was disappointed, but had much to look forward to in his dealings with Junior Laemmle, who wanted to make *Time Out of Mind* and *The Amazing Dr Clitterhouse* with him. The latter story in particular, in which a criminologist turns criminal himself, especially appealed to its potential director.

In the meantime, Whale signed a new deal worth $75,000 a picture with Rogers's 'New Universal'. The studio chief who had pleaded so hard for him to stay was prepared to accept Whale's expensive price tag if he could go on turning out hits. Rogers agreed to Whale's stipulations that he receive his customary 'James Whale Production' credit and be allowed to work on other projects outside the studio. It seemed an ideal situation.

For his first picture under the new deal, Whale decided it was high time he dusted off Sherriff's script for Erich Maria Remarque's *The Road Back*, which had been languishing on Universal's shelves since Junior Laemmle had expressed dissatisfaction with it. Whale, on the contrary, liked Sherriff's adaptation, and entered into pre-production in October 1936.

Remarque's novel followed a handful of the survivors of *All Quiet on the Western Front* as they return to a shattered Germany. For Whale it must have seemed the apotheosis of his war-film reputation: he would outdo his own *Journey's End* and even *All Quiet* – the most popular and successful war film ever made. In addition, Whale wasn't blind to the situation bubbling up in Europe, and warmed to the novel's anti-war themes and dire warnings of the disaffection and resentment brewing in the new Germany.

With the European situation worsening, Universal's fears about the foreign sales of the picture were offset by the domestic business *The Road Back* seemed bound to do. A contemporary newspaper crowed:

Adolph [*sic*] Hitler's hold on Hollywood has slipped completely, it appears with the announcement Universal will super-special *The Road Back*, Erich Maria Remarque's

sequel to *All Quiet on the Western Front*. In case you doubt
the No. 1 Nazi had a very real grip on the film industry, it is
only necessary to recall that Carl Laemmle, former owner of
Universal, held options on this follow-up of one of the largest
box office pictures of all time for four years without doing
anything about it. Remarque, of course, is a fugitive from
Germany because Nazis dislike what is termed 'defeatist'
themes.

Universal had once run a very profitable German arm, which
had fallen apart as the Nazis rose to power. As German influence
spread across Europe, foreign film markets began to shrink and any
perceived slight to the Third Reich or its allies could cause
difficulties for a studio. Indeed, all foreign markets were turning into
minefields. Humphrey Cobb's exposé of French executions, *Road to
Glory*, couldn't find a studio brave enough to take it on: MGM's
proposed version of Sinclair Lewis's *It Couldn't Happen Here* had
been vetoed because its notion of an American fascist regime might
have offended Mussolini or Hitler; and Spain had only recently
succeeded in destroying prints of Von Sternberg's *The Devil is a
Woman*, in which Marlene Dietrich gave an unsympathetic
portrayal of a Spanish girl. Whale, characteristically, didn't give a
damn about such matters, and began shooting in February 1937 on
a budget of $770,000 with a surprisingly lightweight cast, headed by
John King, Slim Summerville, Noah Beery Jnr and the beautiful gay
actor Richard Cromwell. Whale told the *Los Angeles Times*:

When *All Quiet* came out, the names of the actors were not
publicised. It was the story itself that was advertised, and the
success of the story made the actors famous. I think we
should do the same thing with *The Road Back*, not starring
any of the fine actors who will be in it.

As a publicity stunt, the crew were kitted out in German
uniforms appropriate to their status on the film unit. Whale,
resplendent in beret, greatcoat and boots, kept to his costume
throughout the shoot, leading to unfortunate misrepresentations of
his character by the press. Out of his element without the security of

the familiar Laemmles, Whale responded badly to press catcalls and had certain reporters banned from the set, only adding to their scorn.

The weekly status reports of Production Manager Martin Murphy survive, and they give a fascinating indication of Whale's progress and the 'New Universal's' growing disenchantment with him. A week into filming, on 8 February, Murphy refers to Whale as a 'conscientious worker'. Only a week later, on the 15th, he comments on Whale's 'physical and mental condition' as giving cause for concern and the company as working 'very hard'. By the beginning of March he reports progress as 'extremely slow', with the company a full fortnight behind schedule. There is an urgent need to 'speed up Whale', Murphy writes, 'eliminating some of the script' if necessary. 'Whale is the type of director who always wants to put on the screen every hint of the printed script, including punctuation marks.' In Whale's defence, Murphy does admit that a tremendous saving had been made by digging the trenches on the back end of the Universal lot rather than on location.

The budget had now crept up to $850,000 and, by 15 March, Murphy was complaining that Whale was shooting excessive close-ups and unusual angles to 'protect' himself in the editing process. By 22 March, Murphy warned that if the picture were to be brought in under the revised budget estimate (now $880,000), 'Whale will very definitely have to work much faster than he has during any period so far on this production.'

Whale found this level of interference intolerable. He was used to total control, in his films and in life, and found it very hard to work within the unhelpful system at his old studio. Shooting was further delayed by terrible weather and Whale's own contraction of the flu. Already unhappy with progress on what was supposed to be the crowning glory of his career thus far, Whale was then knocked sideways by the actions of the German government. Via their consul in Los Angeles, Dr George Gyssling, the Nazis attempted to shut down the picture altogether. Nothing could be more guaranteed to infuriate Whale. He became more determined than ever to make the film a world-beater, and angrily refused the Nazi's demands. To a Great War veteran, such action on the part of a defeated enemy must have indeed raised hackles.

Not to be put off, Gyssling wrote a letter to twenty of *The Road Back*'s principals:

April 9 1937

With reference to the picture, 'The Road Back', in which you are said to play a part, I have been instructed by my government to issue to you a warning in accordance with Article 15 of the German decree of June 28, 1932, regulating the exhibition of foreign motion picture films.

Copy and translation of this article are enclosed herewith. You will note that the allocation of permits may be refused for films with which persons are connected who have already participated in the production of pictures detrimental to German prestige in tendency or effect in spite of the warnings issued by the competent German authorities.[5]

Germany was, in effect, warning the actors that if they proceeded with the film, their past and future works would be banned in areas of Nazi influence. The ban would extend also to all members of the crew and to Universal itself.

All concerned were outraged and angrily demanded that the US State Department take action against this gross foreign interference. John Emery, who was playing Von Hagen in the picture, wrote for advice as to whether,

as a citizen of the United States, it in future will be incumbent upon me in seeking my livelihood to yield to the pressure which is brought to bear upon me by a foreign consul, acting under the exequatur, and upon the instructions of his government, or whether I can look to the Department of State for help.[6]

Stung by the vehemence of American resentment, Gyssling withdrew, stating: 'I do not intend to carry the matter any further. The letters merely clarified a section of the German law as it applies to screen material exhibited there.'[7] It seemed as though Whale's determination had won the day, but when the film finally wrapped in late April, almost twenty days over schedule and with a budget pushing a million dollars, his position at the 'New Universal' had become very precarious.

The Road Back was previewed in *Life* magazine, who named it their movie of the week. Whale was proud of his work, despite the problems encountered in its making. What happened next amounts to one of the greatest forgotten scandals in Hollywood history.

Despite the vociferous complaints of the State Department, the actors and technicians involved and the American Anti-Nazi League, Charles Rogers and the board of the 'New Universal' decided to cut the film in order to gain German approval. Whether they hoped to offset the film's increased cost by guaranteeing a European distribution or whether they wanted to take Whale down a peg or two, is unclear. Either way, they ordered twenty-one separate cuts, including the film's ending: a hideous dwarf drilling boys in goose-stepping for the *next* conflict that recalled the Hitler Youth. Charles Kenyon was drafted in to write alternative scenes. When Whale refused to direct the new material (mostly weak comic-relief involving the hapless Slim Summerville and Andy Devine), Ted Sloman was brought in to replace him.

The Road Back was wrenched from Whale's hands and emasculated. David Lewis attempted to get David Selznick to intervene, but the effort backfired. Rogers didn't care to have other studios interfering, and Selznick's pleas on behalf of Whale only increased Rogers's anger.

The film, however, still retained some marvellous material. The opening battle scenes are beautifully realized, set against a grim, expressionistic sky. The food riots in the town square, shot from above, are fluid and exciting, and there is a particularly poignant moment in which John Emery emotionally dismisses the last of his battalion, and we see the ghostly comrades who have not returned lining up beside them. What is very clear today is that *The Road Back* was never a *great* film (some weak performances and a muddled attitude to the material ensure that) but it was a *good* one, and Universal's destruction of it remains scandalous. Tragically, only the butchered print survives today.

Left with such a curate's egg, critics were understandably baffled. Those who had read Sherriff's original screenplay recognized that the fault didn't lie with Whale, but for most the broad comedy of some scenes seemed almost obscene next to the grim realities of war presented in others. The California Congress of Parents and Teachers commented: 'The introduction of near slapstick comedy so intrudes upon the seriousness of the theme that it somehow misses the impressiveness which it should have attained.'

Whale could only sit and fume. The film didn't find favour with either the anti-Nazi domestic audience for which it was intended or the Nazi government for whom Universal (founded and, until the year before, run by Jews) had so crassly emasculated it. Whale tried to get out of his contract with his hated new employers, but they would have none of it. The whole experience had been upsetting and miserable, and marked the first occasion he had suffered at the hands of a studio.

Despite all its troubles, *The Road Back* proved to be a major box-office attraction. Sickened, Whale took out a two-page ad in the *Hollywood Examiner*'s preview of the film:

Charles Kenyon
in Collaboration with
R C Sherriff
Wrote the Screen Play for
Erich Maria Remarque's
The Road Back

'Render to Caesar the Things that are Caesar's'

This Page is a Tribute to
R C Sherriff
For His Screen Play and Dialogue
Based on
Erich Maria Remarque's
The Road Back

James Whale

Notes

1. Allan Jones, interview on *Showboat* laser disc (MGM, 1990).
2. 'Showboat', *Picturegoer Weekly*, 1937.
3. David Chierichetti, interview with the author, Los Angeles, May 1994.
4. Donald Bogle, *Toms, Coons, Mulattoes, Mammies and Bucks – An Interpretive History of Blacks in American Films* (Viking Press, New York: 1973).
5. George Gyssling letter, quoted in *Motion Picture Herald*, 19 June 1937.
6. John Emery, letter to US State Department, quoted in *Motion Picture Herald*, ibid.
7. George Gyssling letter, quoted in *Motion Picture Herald*, ibid.

Chapter ten

IRVING Thalberg's tragic and premature death in 1936 had seriously undermined David Lewis's position at MGM. 'You haven't anyone to protect you now,' producer Bernie Hyman told Lewis. 'I'm taking over.' It was, therefore, impossible for the young associate producer to offer James Whale any more work after the disappointment of *Goodbye, Mr Chips*. Eventually, thanks to a party introduction to Jack Warner from his friend Louella Parsons, David Lewis moved to Warner Bros. Anxious for his companion of eight years after *The Road Back* débâcle, Lewis began to actively investigate the possibility of Whale working at Warners. If he could convince the top brass that the failure of the Remarque movie was merely a blip in a career that included hits like *Frankenstein, The Invisible Man* and *Showboat*, then a whole new chapter might well begin for Whale. He was still under contract to Universal for two more pictures but, if things went well at Warners, he could look forward to leaving the bitter experience of *The Road Back* far behind him.

Lewis spoke to Warners' head of production, Hal Wallis, who seemed keen, and then to Mervyn Le Roy, an independent producer who had an agreement with the studio. Le Roy was developing an original screenplay, based on a fictional incident in the life of the legendary actor David Garrick, and thought Whale was just the man to bring it to the screen. Brian Aherne, who was to play the title role, recalled that Ernest Vajda's story was originally enacted to him by Vajda himself in a breathless and hilarious monologue. Aherne maintained that the script was never as funny as this first enthusiastic rendering, but the completed screenplay was nevertheless a delight. The story centred on an elaborate practical joke played on Garrick by the members of the Comédie Française after he has made some ill-advised comments about teaching the French how to act.

The Great Garrick was a very funny script, literate and highly polished and Whale was pleased with it. As well as Aherne, he cast Olivia de Havilland, Edward Everett Horton and Melville Cooper, with old stalwarts Lionel Atwill and the inevitable E E Clive in support. An unknown named Lana Turner appeared some way down the cast list.

Shooting was a happy experience for Whale, even though he was in unfamiliar surroundings. Brian Aherne told the New York Examiner: 'James Whale who directed it, Olivia de Havilland, Edward Everett Horton and the rest of us who played in it seemed to get along like that one happy family that you always read about but never find existing.'

The finished film was very favourably reviewed. The critic Rob Wagner wrote: 'Who says there aren't any new stories? Well, Ernest Vajda thought up a peach for the latest Great Personality picture. ... He has built one of the best stories the screen has ever produced.'[1] Whale's direction was also praised, and the film itself was received as a classy little gem to add to Warners' list of fine films. Unfortunately, as occasionally happens, a well-received film simply fails to take off at the box-office,and this was the case with The Great Garrick. It was especially sad for Whale, in that its commercial failure threatened any second chance that he might have had at Warners. He was still getting his standard $75,000 a picture and the studio couldn't afford another flop.

Whale was seriously disappointed by Garrick's failure. He was, in any case, depressed following the death of his great friend Colin Clive during the shooting of the movie. He must have reflected sadly as to what pass Fate had brought his friend, a scant eight years after their triumph in Journey's End. Clive had become ravaged by alcoholism and appeared terribly skeletal in his penultimate film role, as Jean Arthur's vindictive husband in History is Made at Night (1937). It was during the shooting of this picture that he had broken down and wept hysterically, much to the consternation of the crew. He eventually contracted pulmonary tuberculosis and succumbed to the disease on 25 June 1937 at the Cedars of Lebanon Hospital,

California. Clive's death was a great blow to Whale. Their virtually simultaneous success had encompassed four movies together, during which time they became extremely close. Whale had virtually invented Clive, and his loss must have seemed particularly ominous given the current state of Whale's career. One visitor to the funeral parlour where Clive was laid out was a young man named Forrest J Ackerman, later to found the legendary *Famous Monsters of Filmland* magazine. From the early 1930s, Ackerman had corresponded with Carl Laemmle Snr and was Universal's number one fan:

It was like the beginning of *Bride of Frankenstein* where Clive is sitting up in his dressing gown. You walked into this simple little room and there he was, just like he was asleep. I just stood there and looked at him. My shoulder had brushed his when I was leaving Universal one Summer afternoon in 1935 when I saw the preview of *Bride* at a time when there was rather more to it than was subsequently released. It was a terrible shame. He was a great actor.[2]

Valerie Hobson also recalled Clive's fate with sadness: 'Colin Clive was a strange, quiet, buttoned-up, saturnine sort of man. ... He had a sort of hounded, rather naive quality, like a man who couldn't fight back – whatever his problems were.'[3] James Whale was, as ever, undemonstrative, despite the very real grief he felt at his friend's passing, and absolutely refused to attend Clive's funeral. For one who found such amusement in the ghoulish and unhealthy, he had a very real dislike for the real thing.

Soldiering on, Whale looked forward to his long-planned reunion with Junior Laemmle, who was now working for MGM. Laemmle had lost control of *The Amazing Dr Clitterhouse* to Warners and began, instead, to work on a film based on Marcel Pagnol's *Fanny* trilogy. Preston Sturges had provided the wordy and rather dull script, but Whale hoped that with his old friend as producer he would at last be back in something like his element. It was not to be. Laemmle felt patronized and ignored at MGM and decided he wanted out. Thus, by the time Whale arrived at the studio, he had a new producer, Henry Henigson, and no say over casting.

Although Frank Morgan featured and the delightful Maureen O'Sullivan provided love interest, the film was principally a vehicle for Wallace Beery. Beery was a man's man and took an instant dislike to Whale, referring to him as a 'fairy'. Whale nevertheless ploughed on and finished the picture, which was eventually released as *Port of Seven Seas*.

The Great Garrick, despite its failure, had shown that he could work well outside of the Laemmles' strong patronage. *Port of Seven Seas*, however, had been a whole new proposition. Whale had virtually no control at all and he floundered. Reviews were mixed and business was dreadful. Whale left MGM anxious to put the whole miserable experience behind him.

Unfortunately, he was unable to wipe the slate clean and concentrate on an entirely new approach as he was still contracted to Universal for two more pictures. Charles Rogers and the 'New Universal' board had not forgiven Whale for *The Road Back*, and attempted to buy him out of his contract. It would have been an easy $150,000, but Whale was having none of it. 'They said, "All we have is 'B' pictures," ' Whale later told friends. 'I said, "I love 'B' pictures!" I wanted to sort it out to the last dime.'[4]

Just over a year after finishing the picture which was supposed to be his greatest achievement at Universal, Whale found himself labouring with two dreadful little films: a desert-island potboiler *Sinners in Paradise* and another version of his own *Kiss Before the Mirror*, which became known by the brutally obvious title *Wives Under Suspicion*. Whale's motivation with these two pictures is unclear. He may have been too well aware of his own reputation, or too consummate a professional, to make them deliberately terrible, but his speed in filming seemed more designed to impress than irritate. He finished *Sinners in Paradise* under schedule and under budget, and moved on to *Wives* with even greater alacrity. If he was galled at having to make an inferior version of his own extremely good *Kiss Before the Mirror* then he didn't show it.

The production managers were impressed. On 16 April, they reported: 'It appears to us Mr Whale is endeavouring to prove he can be the fastest shooting director in the organization. His progress on this production for the first week of shooting has been exceptional.' And by 23 April, they were positively bowled over:

> The speed with which Mr Whale is shooting this picture is most unusual. He will finish up tonight four days ahead on our twenty day schedule and from the quality of the daily rushes we honestly do not find his speed will in any way hurt the final product.[5]

Whale, they reported, took great delight in beating their schedule. Despite his impressive work, even on two such low-grade pictures, there was, however, little prospect of a change of heart at Universal. Charles Rogers had been replaced, but the old prejudices remained. Whale took his money and bade goodbye to the studio which had made him.

For the first time in his motion-picture career, Whale had no prospect of further work. He was a wealthy man, thanks to his wise investments and shrewdness (he had engaged Myron Selznick's accountant George Lovett as his business manager). He later confided in a friend that, well aware he was making comparatively huge sums of money, even in the depths of the Depression: 'I realised that it wouldn't last. Right away. And I saved my money right away.'[6] He vividly recalled the experience of Elissa Landi, who had starred for him in *By Candlelight*. She had also appeared in *Sign of the Cross*, and for a brief time was something of a star in Hollywood. Landi and her mother began to throw very lavish parties and at one of these Whale turned to a friend and commented, 'Isn't she a fool. Knowing this won't last.'

Whale was not yet fifty and in no mood to retire. He was a restless, boundlessly creative man and the thought of inactivity appalled him. At home in Pacific Palisades, David Lewis, by then embroiled with the production of Bette Davis's *Dark Victory* at Warners, was anxious to find work for Whale.

In the meantime, Universal was rushing *Son of Frankenstein* into production, after a reissue double bill of *Dracula* and *Frankenstein* had broken box-office records, earning more than on their original release. The man who had given them the original

Frankenstein, its spectacular sequel and Karloff, wasn't even consulted. The film, eventually directed by Rowland V Lee starred Basil Rathbone, Bela Lugosi, Lionel Atwill and Boris Karloff, the latter appearing for the final time as his beloved Monster. *Son of Frankenstein* was splendidly and lavishly realized, but played more like a swashbuckler than a horror film. Such rousing pictures, including Errol Flynn's *Adventures of Robin Hood*, were doing great business and when an offer of work for Whale finally arrived it was in the form of Edward Small's *The Man in the Iron Mask*.

The picture had been adapted from part of Dumas's *The Three Musketeers* by George Bruce. The screenplay was a good one, but unwieldy and way too long. Pruning started as soon as shooting began. Whale always liked to have the script perfect before he shot one frame of film and he found this situation difficult. In principle, the material seemed ideal for him, but as shooting advanced he grew more and more disenchanted. He wasn't particularly happy with the cast (headed by Louis Hayward and Joan Bennett) and became increasingly distant towards them. It was a happier engagement for a young British actor named Peter Cushing, who made his film debut as Louis Hayward's double:

> The two leading male roles were twins, and [Louis Hayward] was cast as both of them. This would involve the split-screen process, and James Whale, the director, wanted an actor who would be willing to play all those scenes with the star, knowing he would never be seen by the public. In editing the final products, the film would be split up the centre, the two Louis Hayward sections stuck together, giving the impression he was playing opposite himself ...
>
> My confidence grew day by day, and to compensate for all my footage which lay cluttering the cutting-room floor, I was given a small part, 'The King's Messenger', which involved me and my attendants in a sword fight with D'Artagnan played by Warren William, and 'The Three Musketeers', played by Alan Hale, Bert Roach and Miles Mander.
>
> 'Ever done any fencing?' asked James Whale.
> 'Oh yes, sir,' said Peter Cushing, 'quite a lot.'

'Good. Go along and see M'sieur Cavern – first-class swordsman. He'll take you through the routine that's been mapped out.'[7]

In fact, Cushing couldn't fence at all and confessed to the Frenchman that he had lied to Whale in order to get the job. Cavern congratulated him on his honesty and promised to make him the best swordsman in Hollywood.

Whale received his statutory fee, his direction credit ('which must be in letters at least 25% as large as the largest letter used in advertising') and his separate credit: 'A James Whale Production'; but he was bored and unhappy. Edward Small interfered wherever possible, in an effort to keep Bruce's wordy screenplay intact. Whale became increasingly detached. The prospect of dismissal loomed large, but Whale seemed not to care. He sat smoking his cigar, letting the smoke drift in view of the camera, bouncing his leg in his familiar fashion. It was not typical behaviour for him and Small found it intolerable.

Whale was fired and George Bruce himself allowed a further nine days filming on his precious script. After all this trouble, the film surprised everyone and became a massive hit. *Box Office* wrote: 'James Whale's direction has a charging pace ... it is probably his best work.' Whale didn't seem to think so, though the film is perfectly good; it is simply devoid of anything which could be called uniquely Whale. In addition to its commercial success, the film was also very well received critically, and some of the Pasadena preview comments survive:

> Mighty fine ... Swell ... Joan Bennett's bowing very poor ... A little too long ... Too much torture ... Lines should be better learned ... More pictures of this type ... Vive la Hollywood! ... Stupendous ... OK ... Gruesome for children ... Fair ... Not as good as a silent picture ... Wonderful, but terrible ...

Whale seemed not to care any more. He wanted to work but his attitude was becoming uncharacteristically cavalier. He had toiled conscientiously on his 'punishment' pictures at Universal, but now seemed content to be fired from a potentially lucrative association with Edward Small. Whale sat back, rather arrogantly, waiting for offers to come in after the huge success of *The Man in the Iron Mask*. Nothing happened. Perhaps rumours had spread that he was becoming difficult to work with. Whatever the reason, Whale returned to Amalfi Drive with no prospect of future employment.

Alan Napier thought Whale's personality may have had more to do with this impasse:

> Jimmy was indeed enigmatic with a taint of sado-masochism in his life-style, which doubtless became more dominant as success adversely affected his career. ... To the English aristocracy in Hollywood, Jimmy never made it. After he stopped making horror films he ceased to exist.[8]

Whale's English reserve was often mistaken for arrogance by his American associates, and it may well be that there was some measure of revenge being enacted in response to his perceived crowing of a few years previously.

It was David Lewis who finally managed to find a new engagement for Whale, a jungle adventure called *Green Hell* which, despite very high production values, is probably one of the worst pictures ever to come out of Hollywood. The screenplay was written by Lewis's friend Frances Marion and concerns the search for lost Inca treasure in the steaming region of Amazonian jungle known as 'The Green Hell'. Douglas Fairbanks Jnr, who headed the cast, was aware of Whale's changing fortunes:

> I don't know why Mr Whale went into decline, but it was very possibly because there were several reports that he was difficult to work with and his employers might well have felt that he was not worth the trouble. I know Mr Whale had a very good reputation. As I recall, some of us in the cast had not thought much of the story, nor indeed of the famous Frances Marion's script. But we were all in one way or another either clients or friends of Harry Eddington, who although normally a most successful agent, was in this case a producer. He approached us on a very personal basis begging

us to make the film at minimum fees and as a special favour to him. It might be that that was also the reason Mr Whale accepted this assignment.[9]

The script was laughably bad, and various members of the ill-fated expedition have to struggle through some tortuously convoluted dialogue:

Richardson: Tell me, Brandon. Is it possible to be in love with two women at the same time, and in your heart be faithful to each, and yet want to be free of both of them?

Whale apparently liked the screenplay, though it is unclear whether he was simply desperate to keep working or planting his tongue firmly in his cheek. Certainly it seems incredible that a personality so full of dark irony could not see that *Green Hell* stank to heaven. Perhaps he hoped to make the whole piece such a romp that people would enjoy the ride and forget the ludicrousness of the script.

Whale assembled old friends around him, including the redoubtable Karl Freund on camera and Ted Kent in the editing suite, and selected an excellent cast, headed by Fairbanks, Joan Bennett, George Sanders and Vincent Price, who later commented, 'It was one of the funniest films ever shot anywhere in the world. About five of the worst pictures ever made are all in that picture.'[10] Douglas Fairbanks Jnr recalled his experience of working with Whale:

My first impression of Mr Whale was during the discussion and pre-production period. I recall him as being very dry, serious, quiet, but definite. I didn't find him a very warm figure to work with. We had no occasion to know each other well away from work. He seemed a bit like the traditional impression of a 'thin-lipped school teacher' ...

... [He] was a bit over-awed by his cast and didn't do very much in the way of altering each one's interpretation and timing. Sometimes, of course, he would make suggestions, but on the whole he was very quiet and seemingly introverted. I heard he had a temper, but I never saw it. I would not venture to call him 'an actor's director'. He seemed thoroughly meticulous and agreeable yet remote.[11]

Desperate for the picture to be a success, Whale had the film previewed in San Francisco, but the reaction was disastrous. The audience laughed out loud and *Green Hell*, an expensive production which eventually cost over $700,000 quickly disappeared to hoots of derision.

Knocked back again, Whale was at a loss to understand what had gone wrong. That the motion-picture industry was a much tougher proposition outside of the Laemmles' secure environment was understandable, but what had he done to deserve such bad luck? His arrogance on *The Man in the Iron Mask* may well have shown he was getting rather difficult, but his very real desire to make even dross like *Green Hell* a success shows that he wanted to keep working. Perhaps he was hoping that another sympathetic production deal might come up, allowing him to work on personal projects closer to his heart.

In 1940, only three years after Universal's capitulation to the Germans over *The Road Back*, Whale found himself involved in an anti-Nazi melodrama for Columbia called *They Dare Not Love*. He wasn't much interested in the film and only received $30,000 for his fee. Whale clashed badly with Columbia's Harry Cohn and even more so with his star George Brent. Also in the cast were Martha Scott and Paul Lukas, but not even the presence of Whale's old friend could make the experience an enjoyable one. Late in January 1941, Whale was told he was being replaced as director by Charles Vidor, who completed the picture and apparently hated every minute of it. Whale's name remained on the credits, however, and the film's poor reception did nothing to help his career. 'Columbia's *They Dare Not Love*', said one paper, 'could have been shelved and no great disaster would have befallen the exhibitors of the country. It is just another (and not top-flight) anti-Nazi picture which is distinguished by poor direction and anemic plot.'

For Whale, *They Dare Not Love* was simply the latest in a depressingly long line of disappointments. If he couldn't have control then he would have nothing to do with Hollywood at all. Enough was enough.

Life had changed very rapidly for both David Lewis and James Whale; but could the former's fluctuating career and the latter's remarkable decline be attributable to Hollywood homophobia? That Lewis was forced from MGM simply because he was gay seems unlikely. He was a favourite of Irving Thalberg, and Thalberg had his enemies. It seems logical, then, that Lewis's sexuality was used as a convenient excuse to remove him once Thalberg's replacements took over.

The situation was probably similar for Whale. Rather than being a victim of direct prejudice, he found others in the industry all too willing to humble him. *The Road Back* was his first real flop, but it showed he wasn't invulnerable. There seemed to be a certain glee shown as Whale's fortunes dwindled so spectacularly. Some movie-people, however, could be spectacularly ignorant, as David Chierichetti recalled:

> One of the big executives at Paramount was a man named Frank Freeman who came from the South. He was often asked to look at films and see if it would offend Southern sensibilities – probably racial things more than anything else.
>
> He once said to a writer, 'I just don't understand that Mitchell Leisen'. And the writer said, 'Well, he's a homosexual.' Freeman said, 'What does that mean?' The writer thought a minute and said, 'It means he has unnatural sexual practices.' And Freeman said, 'What do you mean, he's unfaithful to his wife?'[12]

Without the Laemmles to protect him, James Whale was at the mercy of unsympathetic studio heads who disliked him because he was English, gay and 'aloof'. He had never gone out of his way to socialize with his co-workers, as William Hedgecock, sound recordist on five of Whale's films, testified:

> On the first picture I ever did with the man, he didn't look at me and he didn't speak to me. On the second picture, he

spoke to me but wouldn't look at me. After I'd made four pictures he would look at me *and* talk to me and then I felt as though I'd been accepted.[13]

The director Robert Aldrich, however, always maintained that industry prejudice led to Whale's downfall:

Jimmy Whale was the first guy who was blackballed because he refused to stay in the closet. Mitchell Leisen and all those other guys played it straight, and they were onboard, but Whale said 'fuck it, I'm a great director and I don't have to put up with this bullshit' – and he *was* a great director, not just a company director. And he was unemployed after that – never worked again.[14]

Again and again, however, friends and colleagues testify to Whale's lack of flamboyance, an image totally at odds with the familiar impression handed down by history. Both Jane Wyatt and Gloria Stuart maintain that they didn't discover Whale was gay until years after his death. He was, at all times, reserved and discreet, except perhaps in trusted company when he could afford to relax a little. The explanation, then, seems to lie in the openness of his relationship with David Lewis. This, more than any arch attitude, public display or private scandal, appears to have rankled the homophobic film industry. Certainly, when Lewis was at Warner Bros. he experienced this first hand. Jack Warner disliked Whale intensely and disapproved when he turned up to previews as David Lewis's guest. Finally, Warner spoke to Lewis's agent Phil Berg, who then asked the producer, 'Do you *have* to live with Jimmy Whale?' To which Lewis replied, 'I don't have to, but I want to.'

Notes

1.   Rob Wagner, quoted in *Script*, November 1937, p. 8.
2.   Forrest J Ackerman, interview with the author, Los Angeles, May 1994.
3.   Valerie Hobson, interview with Gregory Mank, Hampshire, 1989; quoted in *Bride of Frankenstein* script book (New Jersey: Magic Image Film Books, 1989).

4.   John Abbott, interview with the author, Los Angeles, September 1993.

5.   Production managers' reports, University of Southern California Archive.

6.   Curtis Harrington, interview with the author, Los Angeles, September 1993.

7.   Peter Cushing, *An Autobiography* (London: Weidenfeld & Nicolson, 1986).

8.   Alan Napier, interview with Gregory Mank; quoted in *Frankenstein* script book (New Jersey: Magic Image Film Books, 1989).

9.   Douglas Fairbanks Jnr, letter to Gregory Mank, 10 April 1982.

10.   Curtis Harrington, interview with the author, Los Angeles, September 1993.

11.   Douglas Fairbanks Jnr, letter to Mank.

12.   David Chierichetti, interview with the author, Los Angeles, May 1994.

13.   John Brosnan, *The Horror People* (London: MacDonald and Jane, 1976).

14.   Vito Russo, *The Celluloid Closet* (New York: Harper & Row, 1981).

Chapter eleven

A SCANT five years after he had crowned his Universal contract with *Showboat*, James Whale had entirely lost interest in motion-picture directing. Restless, bored and increasingly fearful of old age, he might have been completely lost had not David Lewis accidentally hit upon his salvation.

Some time before, despairing of Whale's inactivity, Lewis bought his friend some painting equipment and an easel. Whale was absolutely delighted and found all his old enthusiasm for his previous career returning. It had been many years since he had painted properly and, save for sketched designs for various aspects of his films, he had done precious little drawing. Now, with the brief, charmed period of his directing career apparently over, he felt free to return to his first love. He tried portraits, still lifes and copies of Old Masters with increasing vigour, confidence and success. A little later, he bought some land below the house and had a full studio built.

His style is very attractive: clean, bold colours with a very individual, angular sharpness reminiscent of 1930s advertising posters. One of Whale's best paintings harks back to his glory days in the cinema: it shows Graumann's Chinese Theater on the night of a premiere, the famous building a gorgeous island of colour in a pitch-black night. Patrons are struggling towards the entrance through lashing, impressionistic rain.

At home, Whale's relationship with David Lewis seemed to have settled into a kind of comfortable companionship. Lewis, now almost forty, was becoming rather too old to satisfy Whale's sexual needs. What steps he took to find release for his frustrations are unknown, but John Abbott, who got to know Whale at this time, was aware of the rumours that were circulating:

I'm sure there was no hokey-pokey going on by the time I knew them because Jimmy was looking for other fish to fry. It wasn't wise to talk about people's personal lives in those days. It was very much frowned upon. There were rumours, though. Some of them so absurd. One horrible creature in New York told me he used to have Basil Rathbone but he was *very* expensive! A more unlikely subject than Basil I couldn't imagine.[1]

Whale and Lewis remained extremely fond of each other. With America drifting into war, Lewis joined the air-force and Whale found himself alone. He had his painting, but Amalfi Drive seemed awfully big and empty without Lewis. The outbreak of the Second World War rallied Whale's spirits, however, and he sponsored an orphan via his friend and neighbour Gladys Cooper. He maintained a small circle of friends including Leonore Coffee, Judith Anderson, Philip Merivale, Moyna MacGill and her then unknown daughter Angela Lansbury.

Whale was rather bored, though, and in search of something into which he could channel his talents. Early in 1942, possibly through the absent David Lewis's friendship with Eddie Montagne at RKO, he agreed to direct another film. The title: *Personnel Placement in the Army*, his client: the US military. Many famous directors contributed such instructional films to the war effort, including John Ford who directed a dire warning against the dangers of contracting syphilis.

Whale's film was shot at the Hal Roach studios with Preston Foster, Gordon Jones, Frank Coughlin, Peter Michael and Alan Hale Jnr in the cast. Eddie Montagne was assistant director and fifty soldiers were used as extras. This simplistic propaganda was a far cry from the glory days of Universal, but the patriotic Whale was glad to be of service and the film at least gave him something to do.

Another, far more satisfying avenue for his talents arrived in the same year when he was approached to help entertain the enlisted men who were passing through Los Angeles. Many famous actors gave their services for free, including John Abbott who got to know Whale very well:

I had been at the Old Vic with Olivier in 1936–7 so I knew his then wife, Jill Esmonde. She came out to Hollywood with Tarquin, their son, and she called me up one day and said would I be in this program that Jimmy Whale was doing for the enlisted men out in Brentwood. Well, I was delighted to.

I remembered that, back in London in the late Twenties, I used to pass by the Prince of Wales theatre when *Journey's End* was on and I'd peek in the side-doors when the char-ladies were cleaning it. One day I sat at the back and there was this stage with no lights except the working lights and the simulation of the trenches and stuff. I wasn't an actor then but I came out and saw '*Journey's End* – directed by James Whale' – outside the theatre. And I thought, I wonder who that is?[2]

Whale assembled an extraordinary cast for the show. Gladys Cooper and Philip Merivale did a little sketch called *Two Dogs*, Abbott himself performed in Chekhov's *On the Harmfulness of Tobacco* and *Swansong* (to which Whale gave his blessing), and directed *The Pot-Boiler* with Mercedes McCambridge and George Melville-Cooper. Una O'Connor, Doris Lloyd, Lorraine Day, John Charles Thomas and Alan Jones also took part. Whale himself, as well as designing the sets, directed Harry Morgan in William Saroyan's one-act drama *Hello Out There*. John Abbott recalled the episode:

> He operated the venture with great assiduity, fervency and general enthusiasm. I found him very amenable and very nice. I think he was a frustrated actor. He started rehearsing a little sketch with Eva Gabor, and had David Lewis criticising it on the first night. I didn't think Jimmy was a very good actor.[3]

With Angela Lansbury selling tickets, the whole event became a star-studded occasion and was such a success that it moved to the more spacious Las Palmas Theater in Hollywood. As a result of his performances in Whale's show, John Abbott was offered a part in the movie *Saratoga Trunk* (1943), and credits the experience with opening all the doors for him in Hollywood. A young playwright approached him with an idea for the visiting soldiers, but Abbott didn't think it was quite their cup of tea. Undaunted, the playwright printed his piece, called *Auto-Da-Fé* and dedicated it to Abbott. His name was Tennessee Williams. 'I guess I'm the only actor who ever turned down a Tennessee Williams play,' recalled Abbott. 'But he saw me in Jimmy's show and obviously thought I was right for it.'[4]

During the production, Whale invited John Abbott to Amalfi Drive for dinner, and Abbott later responded in kind:

He used to come to my house quite a bit. Often quite alone. He had a sort of guard but I didn't find him aloof at all. I was aloofer!

He told me very personal things about when Universal tried to break his contract. But he wasn't a flamboyant personality at all. He had a distant kind of inflection in his voice; rather guarded and serious. Not tinged with humour. His voice is not the thing that you remember most. It was like a bank manager's or a school-master's. But he was always immaculately dressed and well behaved. Not at all demonstrative. Not a bit.[5]

At Abbott's dinner parties, Whale would eventually loosen up a little after a couple of drinks. He had no tolerance for alcohol and mostly drank gimlets (gin and lime) which could make him quite garrulous:

He'd tell all these stories about Mrs Patrick Campbell and then have another drink, forget he'd told them and do them all over again. He enjoyed telling one about Mrs Pat's experience at MGM.

Thalberg was doing *Romeo and Juliet* with Leslie Howard and Norma Shearer and they thought it would be a great tribute to Mrs Pat to let her watch the shooting of the balcony scene as she'd been a famous Juliet in her day. Jimmy said they put down the red carpet and sat her down.

When the scene was over, Thalberg brought the stars over to meet her and Mrs Pat said to Norma Shearer, 'Oh, you're so lovely my dear. Such a beautiful skin. Lovely soft hair, oh such pearly, pearly teeth and such *tiny, tiny* little eyes!' And Jimmy would tell that over and over again.[6]

Whale enjoyed these visits as they helped fill up his very empty life without David Lewis, whose companionship he greatly missed. Elsa Lanchester, who saw Whale on and off, commented: 'He was brilliant – such an imaginative mind –but so bitter. And, of course later, he just totally retired from life, save for a few friends – young men and such.'[7] Whale had good cause to be bitter, but few who knew him regarded him as such. He seemed to have no regrets, but he hated getting old and may have endeavoured to keep young company in order to stave off the inevitable. Coincidentally, it was at this time that John Abbott reminded Whale of the young man who had been his lover some fifteen years previously – Robert Barthe Offen: 'I said, "I knew a friend of yours in London, Jimmy. Bobby Barthe." And there was a little pause and he said, "Oh yes. He was a member of the Gallery First-Nighters wasn't he?" He may have been but that wasn't all.'[8]

Reluctant as he was to discuss his private life, Whale's reticence as regards the past was probably more to do with his fear of advancing age. Bobby Barthe was a reminder of happier times, when Whale's career was just about to blossom.

John Abbott's memories provide a picture of a lost soul. 'The fact that Jimmy came up to my house all on his own several times suggests that he was rather a lonely man. I think he'd go anywhere that he was invited.'[9]

Shortly before the end of 1944, Whale made another venture into theatrical direction with Charles K Freedman and Gerald Savory's *Hand in Glove*, a murder thriller about a strangler who frames an innocent idiot for his crimes. The play was set in Yorkshire and featured a diversity of English types whom Whale enjoyed bringing to life. He was back in control, creating the memorable grotesques of his past. Sadly, despite good notices, *Hand in Glove*'s Broadway run was short-lived. Used to disappointment now, Whale slunk back to California, wondering what on earth to do with himself.

David Lewis had continued to prosper, producing *It's a Pleasure* (1945) and *Tomorrow is Forever* (1946) for International/ RKO, and Mitchell Leisen's famous *Frenchman's Creek* (1944) for Paramount. Whale continued to paint and entertain. They had two servants – a cook and a maid called Anna and Johanna (the rhyming names apparently amused Whale greatly) – and gave lavish dinners, but Whale hated living the life of a retired man when he didn't consider himself so.

It was around the time that Lewis was producing one of his greatest hits, the popular Ingrid Bergman/Charles Boyer vehicle *Arch of Triumph* (1948) (ironically based on a book by Erich Maria Remarque) that a new personality entered Whale's life. Curtis Harrington, later to direct such genre favourites as *Who Slew Auntie Roo?* (1971), *Night Tide* (1963) and *What's the Matter with Helen?* (1971) was studying film at UCLA when he got to know Whale:

> As a kid I was a great horror film fan, so for anyone who loves horror films, James Whale has to be right at the top of their list. So it was simply through seeing and admiring *Frankenstein*, *Bride*, *Invisible Man* and especially *The Old Dark House* which is my favourite. I loved his films.[10]

Whale, Lewis and Harrington became great friends and the young student would often be invited up to Amalfi Drive for dinner. Harrington liked Whale enormously and felt none of the coldness so often spoken of in connection with the Englishman:

> I think Jimmy had a natural reserve and dignity and Americans often misinterpret that. If you're not a hundred per-cent 'hail fellow, well met' all the time they think you're being a bit stand-offish, stuck up, so he may very well have created that impression. But if you had a rapport with him like I did ... I never thought of him as cold for an instant. From the first moment I met him, I never felt ill at ease around him in the least. The great thing about Jimmy was his

huge sense of humour. It was delightful, sly and wicked and you see it in all his films. And that's the way he was in real life. He was a great raconteur. He loved his food, his luxuries, his bridge and his cigars after dinner. He lived very, very well in those last years. I think all the heart went out of him when he was given all those 'B' pictures to do. But living well is the best revenge, as they say.[11]

From the start, the two men got on famously, though Harrington found it very difficult to coax anything like a serious comment out of Whale concerning his film work:

He had this disarming, self-deprecating attitude. I'd say, 'Oh, I think *Bride of Frankenstein* is just so wonderful' and Jimmy would say, 'Oh, really? It was just something I did,' and change the subject. What the meaning of that reticence was I really don't know. I do remember asking him, other than horror films, which of his work I would find interesting and he said *Remember Last Night?*. He was very proud of that.[12]

Whale had no interest in any potential new films and had even turned down a contract from David O Selznick for $1000 a week. What he had never considered was television, and when millionaire Huntington Hartford approached him with the idea of filming Saroyan's *Hello Out There*, which Whale had directed for the enlisted men during the war, he accepted.

Hartford wanted to show off the talents of his wife, Marjorie Steele, with whom he was reportedly besotted. Three projects were prepared: Whale's *Hello Out There*, *The Bride Comes to Yellow Sky*, directed by Bretaigne Windust and Joseph Conrad's *The Secret Sharer* directed by John Brahm.

Whale was enthusiastic about the 41-minute film and retained the services of Harry Morgan as the 'Roustabout' – a young man jailed for rape in a small town – who had played the part for him during the war. Phyllis Walker was replaced by Marjorie Steele and the film was prepared for shooting at the KTTV television studios on one set.

Whale didn't enjoy the company of Huntington Hartford, whom he considered rather vulgar. During script meetings, salesmen would come in with boxes of jewellery, push them under the millionaire's nose and ask him to make them an offer. Whale found the whole environment distasteful. He pressed on with the film, however, as Harry Morgan recalled:

> I had great admiration for Jimmy Whale as I'd seen, and loved, so many of his films in the Thirties. I thought the Frankensteins and *The Invisible Man* were just marvellous. Branagh and De Niro? Forget it! When he directed me in *Hello Out There* I found him a very nice person to work with, very cultured. I liked him enormously. We used to rehearse in his beautiful house in the *Palisades* which overlooked the Riviera Golf Course. You went down another level to this magnificent studio and that's where we read the thing through, rehearsed and drank a few gimlets! It was a very pleasant experience all round. I admired him tremendously.[13]

Whale designed the jail set himself and produced an extraordinary construction, clearly derived from his love of German Expressionism: all looming shadows and angled bars. The film itself is extremely interesting, though the performances of both principals are rather broad. Once finished, at a cost of $40,000, *Hello Out There* was shown to a distinguished gathering which included Jean Renoir, William Saroyan, John Huston and Charles Chaplin. Unfortunately, Huntington Hartford was not satisfied with the all-important performance of his beloved Marjorie Steele, and so Whale's last venture, typical of the way his career had declined, was never released. A couple of years later, the other two stories were given a theatrical release as *Face to Face*.

At about this time, Curtis Huntington decided to introduce his friend to a new acquaintance, Christopher Isherwood:

> I thought, here's this world-famous British writer and this world-famous British director living in Hollywood and they really ought to meet. I asked Jimmy if he'd like to meet

Isherwood and he said 'Oh yes, I'd love it' and then I spoke to Isherwood and he said 'Certainly' and so Jimmy invited him to dinner.

When the night came I picked up Isherwood. He was wearing blue-jeans and was already drunk. He was maybe not a fully-fledged alcoholic but he did drink a lot. And he was a very, very unpleasant drunk. Well, the dinner was absolutely disastrous. At that time, I was making short, avant-garde films and Isherwood had seen one and praised it. Jimmy had seen them too. So, more by way of making conversation than anything, we were saying 'Oh, let's make one of Curtis's short films.' Isherwood would be in it and Jimmy Whale would be in it. Isherwood said 'Yes' and looked at Jimmy and said, 'Now I see a scene where you're emerging from a man-hole in the earth!' As though Jimmy were something awful that had crawled out from under a rock! It was such an insult but Jimmy took it with great grace. I was mortified.[14]

Ironically, what the strongly left-wing Isherwood took exception to was the idea of the rich and famous movie-director surrounded by such opulence. Had he known of the grim, working-class poverty in which Whale had been brought up, his behaviour may have been somewhat different.

As the years went by, Whale found it increasingly difficult to keep himself busy. He seemed unsure about what might occupy him best, and turned down a contract from producer William Dozier to film Wells's *The Food of the Gods* through sheer indifference. One area which seemed to hold some interest for him was the theatre, and he returned to it in 1950 when approached to direct a comedy called *Pagan in the Parlour* by Franklin Lacey. Whale directed a production at the Pasadena Playhouse in February 1951 and then arranged to take the play home to England. Curtis Harrington had by then moved to Paris, but had been aware for some time that all was not well between Whale and Lewis:

He and David were lovers for years but that was a long time before I met either of them. By then, they were more companions than lovers. I really don't know what went wrong with their friendship. I can only assume it was attrition.[15]

With nothing to do, Whale's creative energies were turning in on themselves, and he became irritable and difficult. He needed to get away and the trip to Europe sounded ideal. Leaving Lewis behind, Whale caught a boat to France. Arriving in Paris, he looked up Curtis Harrington who was living pretty much hand-to-mouth, subsidized by occasional twenty-dollar bills from his parents. The prevalent black market was very favourable to dollars and he managed to get by, living in a bohemian style which pleased him:

> I could manage to go to cheap Left-Bank restaurants and stay in little Left-Bank hotels. But when Jimmy arrived he stayed in a *grand* hotel and he took me to some *very* grand restaurants.
>
> One night, we dined out in a very nice place at the edge of the Seine and as we were parting company he suddenly reached into his wallet and pulled out something like twenty thousand francs. It seemed like a fortune to me. He pressed it into my hand and said, 'Here. I admire you so much for having the courage to come here and expand your life this way. I know it must be tough on you financially and if this can help, this is just a little something from me.' It was just a spontaneous kindness and I've never forgotten it.[16]

Whale's interest, as ever, was in younger men and, at the age of sixty-one, he was becoming increasingly sexually tormented: his snow-white hair and lined face belying the youthful energy which surged within him. Harrington picked him up for breakfast one morning and Whale confessed to having spent the night with a young man: ' "Oh I spent the most wonderful night," Jimmy told me. "I feel like I'm twenty-five again." He felt this tremendous surge of youthful vigour.'[17]

Whale knew few people in Paris except Harrington, and one night during his stay he met a 25-year-old man from Strasburg named Pierre Foegel, who was acquainted with the owners of the bar in which Whale was drinking. The two men got along well, despite Foegel's limited English (his studies in Paris had been interrupted by the German Occupation) and soon after, Whale offered him a job, principally as his chauffeur:

> They told me he was a movie director but the job he offered was no big deal. I was young and when someone says, 'Hey, wanna go to Italy?' what do you do? I thought it was a good opportunity. It was like a paid vacation.[18]

From Paris, they drove in a Citroen which Whale had bought, first to Milan, then Rome and Venice and finally through the tunnel to Switzerland. Most of the time was spent in galleries and museums, where Whale studied the works of other painters. He talked a little of location-scouting for films, though he can't have meant this very seriously.

In Rome, Whale was armed with some letters of introduction which gained them entry to the Vatican where, on Easter Sunday, they were taken to the diplomatic balcony and saw the Pope. Undoubtedly, they were pampered in some places because of Whale's name and reputation. Whale and Foegel's friendship grew apace and when they crossed over to England for the production of *Pagan in the Parlour*, Foegel's duties were extended to include cleaning, cooking and general household tasks. Whale rented a flat in Knightsbridge and began rehearsals with a cast which included a young Joss Ackland:

> *Pagan in the Parlour* was a big blockbuster of a show under the management of Lord Vivian who had just taken over from C B Cochran. [It] starred Hermione Baddeley as a cannibal without a word of English, who bounced around going 'ugga-wugga'. The other stars were Moyna MacGill, the mother of Angela Lansbury and daughter of George, the politician. The lush settings were by Doris Zinkeisen and, after a six-week tour, it was planned to take the show to London and then New York.[19]

Ackland was delighted to work with Whale, whom he liked and respected. *The Old Dark House* had always been one of his favourite movies. *Pagan in the Parlour* opened to record business at the Theatre Royal in Bath and then transferred to the Wimbledon Theatre in London.

After dropping Whale off every morning, Foegel would return to the apartment and clean up, cook dinner and then return for Whale if they weren't spending the evening out. Sometimes he would visit the theatre, and found himself required to stand in on more than one occasion:

> I knew all the lines for one of the boys. When he wasn't feeling good I could understudy. I learned the part but not to go on the stage, just to replace him if he wasn't well. As a stand-in I could it. I think I knew *Pagan* off by heart. I was doing everything. I was Man Friday![20]

Whale spent a lot of time with his old friend Doris Zinkeisen and had high hopes for the play's success. Joss Ackland, however, sadly recalled the show's progress:

> As the weeks went by it became clear that *Pagan* would never reach London or New York. Hermione Baddeley grew frustrated saying nothing but 'ugga-wugga' and managed, at one performance, to get in a 'not bloody likely!' After one dreary matinee, as we took the curtain calls she stepped forward and told the audience that they should be ashamed of themselves for not laughing more. 'We work hard up here,' she said. 'The least you can do is try and co-operate!' All the pensioners seated out front looked confused and stared blankly at each other, as we could hear Lord Vivian rushing angrily backstage, through the auditorium.
>
> James Whale and Moyna MacGill soon returned sadly to Hollywood and the rest of us went back to the breadline.[21]

Before his return to America, Whale was flattered to be asked to attend an evening in his honour at the British Film Institute. This came about through Curtis Harrington's friendship with Gavin Lambert, the editor of *Sight and Sound*:

Jimmy was quite flattered by it, I know. It was quite unexpected. We found a beautiful print of *The Old Dark House* and ran it in London and there was a wonderful reaction. Jimmy was terribly pleased but always very modest about his accomplishments and his films, in the tradition of a gentleman who says, 'Oh you know, it was nothing.'[22]

After the failure of *Pagan in the Parlour*, this tribute must have pleased Whale but there was no prospect of any future work.

Pierre Foegel came to stay with Whale in California from January to June 1953 after which he went back to France. The two men corresponded and, after Whale had sent him the relevant papers, Foegel returned to California for good in January 1954. His relationship with David Lewis had deteriorated completely, and Whale asked him to move in to the studio to make room for Foegel, probably well aware how his old lover would react. Lewis, not unexpectedly, moved out and Foegel arrived a short time later. Despite the abrupt and hurtful nature of their parting, Whale and Lewis remained very good friends and Lewis was a frequent visitor to the house.

Meanwhile, Whale and Foegel continued to get along. Whale seemingly revitalized by his youthful companion. He settled into a routine, characteristically in complete control of his environment, as Foegel recalled:

He was very private about his earlier life. I got the feeling that somewhere along the line he got hurt by somebody. We never discussed it.

His life was pretty much on a schedule. He'd get up about 7.30 or so and the maid brought him orange juice. Then he had breakfast and went down to his studio and stayed there till lunchtime. At one, the maid would call him up and he'd have cold cut and salad for lunch with a bottle of beer which he drank out of a silver goblet. He was very particular about keeping his beer cold.[23]

Foegel spent an initial five months at Amalfi Drive, deciding whether or not to make the momentous decision to emigrate. During this time, he badgered Whale to have a swimming pool installed opposite the studio:

> I must've put the bug in his ear. One day he called somebody and by Christmas there was a new pool. I was the first one to take a dive in it. He would go in and walk around but he couldn't swim. I used it on almost a daily basis.
>
> Once in a while on a weekend we had some people round for a pool party, maybe David Lewis, Buddy Nolan and some friends. When you've got a pool you get a lot of people dropping in on a hot day![24]

Foegel returned to France in June 1953 and continued to correspond with Whale. It was during his absence that Whale began to throw the 'Babylonian' parties which were later to contribute to his scurrilous and undeserved reputation. These 'pool parties' were attended almost exclusively by young gay men whom Whale seemed desperate to impress. He was an old man, though, and the company of such people could only increase his sense of alienation.

Pierre Foegel, not surprisingly, decided that the standard of living was somewhat better in California and, after Whale arranged all the relevant papers, returned to Amalfi Drive in January 1954. This, Whale told him, was the chance of a lifetime. Shortly afterwards, Foegel began to study English at UCLA:

> When I came back he said, 'Ok, what do you want to do?' So I went to work in a department store as a salesman and about a year later I took over a gas station on Third Street.
>
> He was a very cool man, very phlegmatic but it was important not to rock the boat. He could get pretty mad and it took us a long time to get together on some things. I liked to argue points but with him, at first, his word was law. He could be sharp. Even cutting. If I did something wrong he'd say, 'If I'd done it like that I'd kick myself'. It was the tone of his voice more than anything else. It could get icy cold and when I heard that icy voice running down my back I knew I was in trouble! But there was no animosity. It was done and it was over. That's what I liked about the man. We did have

a joke though. Never discuss religion or politics unless you want a fight![25]

Whale's coolness was put to the test one night when the garage containing Foegel's 1947 cadillac and Whale's 1954 Ninety-Eight convertible caught fire. The tank of the cadillac was full and the whole lot exploded:

> I ran into the house and got a big suitcase and threw all my papers in there: passport, immigration, everything and threw them on the lawn in back. I grabbed the garden hose and poured water on the burning cars. Jimmy walked up to me with a box of cigars under his arm and said, 'You got a light?'[26]

Whale seemed happy and settled. Those who knew him maintain that he bore no bitterness over the decline of his career, he was simply glad that it had lasted as long as it did and he was able to live so well. After his day in the studio, Whale would discuss the evening's dinner with the cook, which would be served at seven. He drank two gimlets, which had to be made one at a time with fresh ice for each glass straight from the freezer. He continued to entertain, holding court and telling stories while smoking one of his enormous cigars. He was very close to Doris Lloyd and her sister Milba, while other visitors to Amalfi Drive included Mae Clarke, Angela Lansbury, Alan Napier, Gladys Cooper and Judith Anderson. Charles Laughton and Elsa Lanchester came to dinner occasionally and once, memorably, reciprocated the invitation. Pierre Foegel remembered the evening well:

> Jimmy was in his tuxedo and I had a beautiful new suit. We spent a long time getting dressed. I remember standing in front of the mirror doing my tie for what seemed like forever. Anyway, we drove round and their very English butler answered the door. We went in – so formal – and there was Laughton in a Hawaiian shirt! In came Elsa Lanchester wearing what they call a Mou-Mou: a great long dress right down to her ankles.

I was furious but Jimmy thought it was terribly funny. After that, we went down to their pool and Jimmy and Laughton sat talking. I went for a swim and had to borrow some trunks. Not Laughton's though![27]

Whale and Laughton discussed plans for another project, an operetta based on the writings of Max Beerbohm and Ray Bradbury which would feature Elsa Lanchester.

Whale enjoyed driving, and he and Foegel would motor out to the Biltmore Hotel in Santa Barbara for lunch about three times a month. They visited San Francisco, where Whale posed in front of the Buddha in the famous Japanese tea garden. Foegel remembered with amusement the day Whale decided to buy a new car:

Jimmy wanted this car he'd seen and it was on some lot or other so he went down to talk to the salesman. Anyway, this guy wasn't too helpful and Jimmy didn't like his tone so he went away and spoke to George Lovett, his business manager and he bought the car lot! A couple of days later he went down and said to the guy, 'OK, I'm your boss now. How much for the car?'[28]

Although Whale was very fond of Pierre Foegel, the Frenchman wasn't popular with some of Whale's older friends. Many felt he was simply using Whale, despite the hard work he did and the obvious affection he held for the ageing director. Curtis Harrington found that he was no longer invited to Amalfi Drive, a fact he blamed on Foegel's increasing influence. This seems extremely unlikely considering Whale's mania for control over his own life.

One night, late in 1956, Whale and Foegel were having dinner as usual when Whale's face became flushed:

I asked him what was the matter and he didn't answer for a few seconds and then he said, 'I'm alright, its passing.' Then he went into the living room and watched TV.

He saw his doctor a couple of days later and seemed to be alright but he'd definitely had a stroke of some sort. About three weeks later something snapped in his mind. I wasn't in the house but he walked downstairs stark naked and mumbled something to the girls.[29]

Unable to reach Foegel, the maid called David Lewis who was over at MGM working on *Raintree County* with Elizabeth Taylor and Montgomery Clift. By the time Lewis arrived, Whale had been admitted to St John's Hospital where he was treated for a nervous breakdown, and given shock treatment.

After a while, Foegel took in Whale's portable easel to the sanitorium, but Whale was no longer sufficiently in control to paint: 'He didn't mix the colours any more. There was no detail. He painted a coffin once. It was red and black. The proportions and the perspectives were right but the colours were straight out of the tube.'[30]

Whale valued control above all things and the prospect of life as a spoon-fed invalid filled him with horror. He couldn't paint any more and his reading suffered. In the middle of 1957, allowed home from the convalescent hospital, he decided to take control of the one thing left to him: his death.

Memorial Day, 29 May, was a public holiday. Whale gave his nurse the day off, promising to take his own medication. Pierre Foegel recalled the events of that day with great emotion:

Jimmy kept everything inside. Never talked to anybody about it. If he had I'd have said to the doctors, you'd better get this guy under twenty-four-hour surveillance, which he more or less was anyway. But when he gave the nurse Memorial Day off he was acting normally. He even fooled me. I wasn't going to have the gas station open all day anyhow. It was a holiday. So I said I'd go down and check everything and lock up early. There wouldn't have been any business anyway. But he fooled me. He seemed to be progressing.[31]

Whale had his breakfast as usual and, dressed in his favourite suit, wandered down to the studio. His plan was carefully formulated. He took out some paper and wrote a long note:

To ALL I LOVE,

Do not grieve for me – My nerves are all shot and for the last year I have been in agony day and night – except when I sleep with sleeping pills – and any peace I have by day is when I am drugged by pills.

I have had a wonderful life but it is over and my nerves get worse and I am afraid they will have to take me away – so please forgive me – all those I love and may God forgive me too, but I cannot bear the agony and it is best for everyone this way.

The future is just old age and pain. Goodbye all and thank you for all your love. I must have peace and this is the only way.

Jimmy

Perhaps his nerve failed him a little here as he looked out towards the pool. At any rate, he added a lengthy PS:

Do not let my family come – my last wish is to be cremated so nobody will grieve over my grave – no one is to blame. I have wonderful friends and they do all they can for me, but my heart is in my mouth all the time and I have no peace. I cannot keep still and the future would be worse. My financial affairs are all in order and I hope will help my loved ones to forget a little. It will be a great shock but I pray they will be given strength to come through and be happy for my release from this constant fear. I've tried very hard all I know for a year and it gets worse inside so please take comfort in knowing I will not suffer any more.

J

He wrote 'To Those Whom I Love' on an envelope and slipped the folded note inside. He left the studio, and walked towards the pool. There would be one last flamboyant gesture from this uncommonly reserved man. He was not the kind to slip away with pills. Sometime before one o'clock, James Whale threw himself into the shallow end of the pool and struck his head against the bottom. He had left a book on his bedside table. With a wry irony which he must have planned, it was called *Don't Go Near the Water*.

Pierre Foegel vividly recalled his frantic ride back to Amalfi Drive:

> I was at the gas station and some time after one o'clock the maid called me and said, 'Mr Whale is in the pool'. I said, 'Let him have fun. Let him enjoy himself.' And she said, 'But you don't understand, he's on the *bottom* of the pool.'
>
> I jumped in my car and drove like a goddamned maniac. I picked up George Lovett from his office on La Cienaga and got to Beverly Hills at sixty mph. I hit ninety on San Vincente and sixty on Sunset. I took the turn onto Amalfi on two wheels. It took me twenty-two minutes. We ran through the house and down to the lower level. I took off my shoes, jumped into the pool and brought Jimmy's body up. There was a bump on his forehead above his eye. Just a bruise. By the time I got his body on the side of the pool the firemen arrived and then I just *went*. I just sat down and let them take care of it and went into shock. George Lovett found the note but he only let me read half of it. I guess he figured it wasn't for me to know.[32]

In those days, the stigma of suicide was very real and a decision was taken to keep the note secret. Lovett showed it to David Lewis who took care of the funeral arrangements.

Whale was cremated on 3 June 1957 at Kingsley and Gates Mortuary Chapel, South Sepulveda Boulevard. A niece and nephew flew in from England to attend. Also present were old friends Doris and Milba Lloyd, George Lovett and his sister Hilda Walls, Carl Laemmle Jnr and, of course, David Lewis and Pierre Foegel. Judith Anderson read the lesson, the twenty-third psalm, and afterwards Whale was interred in niche 20076 in the Great Mausoleum, Forest Lawn, Glendale.

Notes

1. John Abbott, interview with the author, Los Angeles, September 1993.
2. Ibid.
3. Ibid.
4. Ibid.
5. Ibid.
6. Ibid.
7. Elsa Lanchester, interview with Gregory Mank, Los Angeles, 1979; quoted in *Bride of Frankenstein* script book (New Jersey: Magic Image Film Books, 1989).
8. Abbott, interview with the author.
9. Ibid.
10. Curtis Harrington, interview with the author, Los Angeles, September 1993.
11. Ibid.
12. Ibid.
13. Harry Morgan, interview with the author, September 1993.
14. Harrington, interview with the author.
15. Ibid.
16. Ibid.
17. Ibid.
18. Pierre Foegel, interview with the author, Los Angeles, May 1994.
19. Joss Ackland, *I Must Be In There Somewhere* (London: Hodder & Stoughton, 1989).
20. Foegel, interview with the author.
21. Ackland, *In There Somewhere*.
22. Harrington, interview with the author.
23. Foegel, interview with the author.
24. Ibid.
25. Ibid.
26. Ibid.
27. Ibid.
28. Ibid.
29. Ibid.
30. Ibid.
31. Ibid.
32. Ibid.

Chapter twelve

JAMES Whale's estate amounted to over $600,000 at the time of his death, and his will decreed that one-sixth should each go to David Lewis and Pierre Foegel. Specific bequests of £1,000 went to Una O'Connor, Gladys Cooper, Doris Lloyd and Doris Zinkeisen, with the remainder going to Whale's family.

George Lovett took control of the James Whale Company until his death in 1964, after which his sister Hilda Walls assumed responsibility until her own death in 1978. The California Superior Court appointed William E Guthner trustee in 1979 and he handled the company until it was eventually wound up in the late 1980s. The trust had not been very well handled, with several dubious shares and pieces of uninspiring property purchased in its name. All concerned, however, had reason to be grateful to James Whale for many years after his death.

For some time afterwards, there were ugly rumours of foul play, as Pierre Foegel was suspected of having assaulted Whale. Another story of near-legendary proportions spoke of Whale's murder at the hands of a beautiful boy whose nude portrait he had been painting. Equally lurid tales began to circulate of the infamous director whose outrageous lifestyle and flamboyant sexuality had led to his Shelley-esque demise; of how his homosexuality – his own personal Frankenstein monster – had destroyed him. All of which was a long way from the sad and moving end of the sensitive and brilliant man James Whale actually was.

The suicide note was turned over to David Whale after George Lovett's death, and he kept it safe until he himself died of respiratory complications in 1987. Pierre Foegel, retired after a successful career as a chef, lives today in Sepulveda Boulevard, Los Angeles:

For two or three years after I even denied that it was suicide because I didn't want his memory sullied. I'd say it was an accident. I was in mourning for at least ten years.

How do I regard him after all these years? As a very dear friend. I say hello to him. I go to Forest Lawn with a flower every now and then. I surrounded myself with the paintings and the furniture. Like a shrine, A James Whale museum. He taught me self-control. Always be in control of yourself. Believe in what you're doing and go after it.[1]

James Whale's quest to reinvent himself succeeded far better than he could ever have dreamed: The 'Would-Be Gentleman' became a true gentleman: respected, loved by those who truly knew him and, after all these years, rightly acknowledged as a superb film-maker.

Just before Whale died, he wrote a letter to his old friend John Rowe, expressing his joy at his brother's discovery of family documents relating to seventeenth-century members of the Whale clan. They had been, it appeared, considerable landowners and 'gentlemen'. 'I cannot help a feeling of comfort in my old age', wrote James Whale, 'that I was born right.'[2]

Notes

1. Pierre Foegel, interview with the author, Los Angeles, May 1994.
2. Peter Barnsley, 'Mystery Man', *The Black Countryman*, Summer 1969.

Appendix

THE following is the original proposal for *The Invisible Man* which James Whale wrote in early 1932.

THE INVISIBLE MAN
By
James Whale
(Star – Karloff)
Jan. 3, 1932

An important personage lies dying in a magnificent bedchamber. Priests, doctors and relatives group themselves, grimly mourning, so deeply we possibly suspect treachery.

Hope is abandoned, priest is about to administer last sacrament, when one of the servants rushes in, breaks through the group and says if only his master would permit his doctor he knows he could cure him. The mourners are outraged, and start to bully him out, when the dying old man notices the commotion, demands to know what it is. An evil looking doctor tells the dying man it is only a poor, crazed servant who wants to bring some quack doctor into his presence. Upon further insistence the servant is brought to the foot of the bed, in much the same manner as an early martyr, surrounded by priests etcetera. The old man motions for them to let him speak. The servant tells his tale. He doesn't know who he is, but a strange, tall, thin man whose face no one has ever seen tends all the poor of the village, and refuses payment. He is surrounded by mystery. They think he is expatiating some dreadful sin, and the villagers call him the invisible man.

Horror and consternation in the bedchamber! They are about to fall on him and drag him from the room, when the old man in a weak voice orders that the doctor be brought.

They drag the servant out of the room, pull him down the stairs, throw him on the floor of the hall, and bully him more than ever. The peasant, now having the backing of his master, suddenly takes on a new authority, and makes his own conditions. He must be driven alone to a spot he will point out, and no one will be permitted to go to the doctor's abode. A conveyance and driver are brought, and they clatter off into the night.

A few shots of weird aspect brings us to a lonely spot on the outskirts of the town.

The servant suddenly cries, 'Stop!' The driver pulls up suddenly, and is about to get down, but is mysteriously prevented from doing so by the servant who says; 'Everything depends on your being blind and deaf – stay here and do nothing until I return.'

We follow the servant through weird gates past shadowy trees, expecting to come upon a strange house, but instead he hops over a wall into a queer bleak churchyard, with gleaming crosses, and grim ghostly monuments.

He comes at length to a dark family vault with iron railings, in which is a little gate, which he opens an passes through, looking round however furtively before doing so. Standing in the middle of the enclosure is a monument, somewhat like an upturned sarcophagus, tall and grim, an exquisitely carved angel's head with spreading wings is at the top. Taking up a heavy stone the servant knocks three times on the grave, making a horrid sickening noise. There is silence for a moment, and we hear a slight subterraneous rumble, followed a moment later by a voice from nowhere. 'Who are you?'

Servant mumbles his name accompanied by two rapid knocks and we hear more rumblings coming up from the earth. The servant now stands upright in front of the monument expectantly.

CAMERA FOCUSES on the angel's beautiful face, which slowly hinges outwards, revealing a dim, vague, but horrid shape in the aperture, framed on either side by the two delicate angel's wings.

The face in the aperture is very startling. It is wrapped entirely in bandages, rather like a mummy, and wears a pair of heavy dark glasses. It moves and speaks: 'Well, William, what is it?'

Whereupon the servant begs him to come and see his master, adding, it is a matter of life and death. The voice which is very beautiful, sardonically replies:

'It is always a matter of life and death. – Come in.'

We have now the thrill of introducing a mysterious BEING of the Dracula and Frankenstein order, but with the difference of meeting what is obviously a delightful person behind that cryptic makeup.

The lid of the sarcophagus opens mysteriously and both the stranger and the servant disappear into the bowels of the earth. The lid of the sarcophagus closes and the CAMERA PANS up to the smiling expression on the angel's sweet face as the picture FADES . . .

AS AN ALTERNATIVE SUGGEST INSTEAD OF A FADE WE COULD GO IN. The stranger switches on an electric torch, leads the way followed closely by the servant, both disappearing into the bowels of the earth.

THE CAMERA anticipates their entrance into what is obviously an old family vault. The walls of the interior are lined with coffins, resting on marble slabs. In the centre of the chamber lies another casket, on which are strewn a few magazines a papers, and which serves as seat and table.

The stranger gracefully indicates for his visitor to be seated, apologizing for lack of modern comforts, and for the magazines which are slightly out of date. There is a very short scene, and with charming manners, which however have a firm authority behind them he asks to what he owes the pleasure of this visit. The peasant tells of his master, who is a good man, lying at the point of death, being slowly murdered by poison, or starvation, and we learn that the servant's wife and child were miraculously cured by the mysterious stranger, who leaves the peasant for a moment and disappears behind another door, into what will ultimately be the laboratory of invisibility, but which we do not see now.

He reappears however very shortly, with hat, stick, and a small bag, and as they exit . . . we DISSOLVE BACK into the sick bedchamber.

There is much commotion in the house. The doctors and relatives are all there insisting the old man take further doses of their medicine, but he weakly waves them away. They are just about to overcome his reluctance however when the priest says:

'Listen!'

There is silence and we hear the rumble of the carriage wheels. They rush to the window and there is considerable suspense, as the carriage stops, and the servant alights, alone, shutting the door after him. We watch him from above coming up the steps of the house, and disappearing under the lens of the camera.

The crowd all rush to the door of the bedroom and after a little suspense it opens, and the servant enters. He gives some instructions from the invisible man which are, they must all leave the room and passages quite clear. After some protest this is done.

The stranger is now brought in to the house by the servant. His entrance is full of mystery and we avoid shots of his face. The CAMERA being either behind, or at such an angle it accentuates the weirdness of the mysterious figure. They cross the hall, mount the great staircase, stand for a moment outside the bedroom. The stranger asks if his instructions are carried out, and they enter.

The CAMERA still following them into the huge bedroom. The firelight is flickering with ghostly effect. No sound is heard except perhaps the ticking of a clock, or the bark of a dog.

The CAMERA moves swiftly to a CLOSE UP of the old man, and we discover he has been blindfolded. Into the shot the stranger's expressive hands feel pulse, take temperature, etcetera. As we hold on to the old man the hands go out of the shot, and mix certain medicines. The old man's breathing is very laboured and somewhat ghastly, one of the stranger's hands gently raises the old man's head, and with the other gives him the mixture. Hands go out of the picture, puts down the glass, and gently lays the head back on the pillow. After a moment's sympathetic caress the hands undo the bandages, and we discover the old man's eyes have closed, his breathing has become easier, and he peacefully sleeps.

Still keeping the stranger's back to the camera we see him collect his props and perpare to leave, before he does so however, something dramatic must happen to the invisible man, and our story must develop. It might be that the daughter who has remained, concealed in the room, rushes forward dramatically, and tearing off the stranger's cloak and hat, demands to know who he is.

It is child's play to snatch a tense moment here, as the gruesome face savagely turns upon her and looks into the CAMERA.

In a weirdly tender scene the girl might here discover her lover, who had mysteriously disappeared, because of a horrible disfigurement to his face during scientific experiments for the good of the poor sick. After a heartbreaking scene she enters the most exclusive order of nuns in a convent, and banishes herself from the world.

The stranger returns to his tomb, and in an agony of spirit, wrestles with God. His hands clasped in religious fervour, he prays:

OH THOU WHO ART INVISIBLE
and to whom nothing is unseen
who carest for the sick and fatherless,
who created the earth and all that is upon
it, to whom there is no mystery in man or
beast: THOU who gavest and takest away, hear
the prayer of thy servant, and remove from
the eyes of mortal man the harmful sight of
this frightful face, that I may be allowed
to do thy will useen

At the end of the prayer, which is terrible in its intensity, the music, which has accompanied the entire picture in the grand opera manner, swells into something like an aria, 'Oh turn me not away from thy compassion'.

After much research he works out his own answer to the prayer, and gets to the point of making himself invisible in the great experiment scene. Standing before the grim apparatus we lead up to the slow unwinding of his bandages, revealing for the first time in his features a horror so fantastic, so unbelievably hideous, that although he deals with the devil himself, we sympathize with his desire to become invisible. With the old servant as an accomplice, and with all the arts of Camera and mystery trickery, the stupendous achievement is complete, but our horror grows as we discover that during the transition the mind has completely changed, and now has only a longing to kill those people he had healed and befriended.

His first victim is the poor, crazed servant and we FADE OUT on the delightful spectacle of his being slowly strangled to death by invisible hands. As a crowning piece of horror and before the death rattle of the victim announces his demise, the stranger's horrible face, which now has the added terror of a murderous mind, becomes visible in the victim's last fleeting moment from this beautiful world. Having been suspended in the air the victim falls dead on the floor, with a face of frozen horror. The corpse receives a violent kick from an invisible foot, and our CAMERA panning down, traces footsteps of naked feet, treading in blood, to the door. Coming up to the door handle we hear a squeak, and the door opens of its own accord, almost immediately however, closing to the accompaniment of soft laughter, dying away as the invisible man FADES OUT in to the lovely night.

If this is too mild the corpse could be lifted by invisible hands, dragged swiftly out, and flung either on to a grave in the churchyard, or into a still farther recess in case we wish to pile future corpses into a funeral pyre.

A short series of diabolical murders is planned and executed.

Meanwhile the lovelady is about to take her final vows to enter the most exclusive order of Sisterhood. In this scene which offers scope for magnificent production, the splendour of the ceremony of consecration could be researched for impressive details.

Knowing that the invisible man is on her track, we could build suspense by having the most elaborate presentation. The acolytes could trim the altar, priests, processing back and forth with all the ritual stressed. The procession of nuns with swinging censors, the novices prostrate in white on the steps of the altar. The clanging of the bells and the peal of the organ. The CAMERA, which is now on the face of the holy bride, exquisitely sad, and spiritually beautiful, PANS swiftly across the Cathedral to a door, which slowly opens. A knife stealthily creeping towards the altar, accompanied by soft footfalls of naked feet. The knife furtively passes in and out of the pillars, and eventually comes to a stop, setting high up in the great carved chair of the Bishop.

We cut several times during the ceremony to this playful knife, somewhat in the nature of the hand on the bannisters in *The Dark House*, and as the lovely bride is receiving the sacrament, the knife raises and completes its bloody work.

Our meal of horror is not yet complete. The liqueur is still to be served. Our eyes must surely pop completely out as we watch the knife jerk itself free from the now unlovely corpse, raise itself into mid-air, and plunge itself quivering into the heart of the remorseful invisible man. Who, as his life's blood ebbs swiftly away, becomes gradually visible, revealing for an instant, a face so fantastically horrible that even we who are used to such dishes, close our eyes, as the sound of a dull flopping thud forces the sickening news through our other senses, that the lovers are united at last!

Finis

Reproduced by permission of Hollywood Publishers, Universal City, CA.

Bibliography

Ackland, Joss. *I Must be in there Somewhere* (Hodder and Stoughton, 1989)

Balcon, Michael. *A Lifetime of Films* (Hutchinson, 1969)

Browne, Maurice. *Too Late to Lament* (London: Victor Gollancz, 1955)

Cushing, Peter. *An Autobiography* (Weidenfeld & Nicholson, 1986)

Curtis James. *James Whale* (Scarecrow Press, 1982)

Drinkwater, John. *The Life and Adventures of Carl Laemmle* (New York: G. P. Putnam's Sons, 1931)

Gielgud, John. *Early Stages* (London: Macmillan, 1939)

Lanchester Elsa. *Charles Laughton and I* (London: Faber & Faber, 1938)

Lanchester, Elsa. *Elsa Lanchester Herself* (Michael Joseph, 1983)

Lewis, David. *The Creative Producer* (Scarecrow Press, 1994)

Mank, Gregory William. *It's Alive!* (San Diego: A. S. Barnes and Co., 1980)

Morley, Sheridan. *Tales from the Hollywood Raj* (Weidenfeld and Nicholson, 1983)

Parker, Peter. *Ackerley – The Life of J. R. Ackerley* (London: Constable & Co., 1989)

Pearson, George. *Flashback* (George Allen & Unwin, 1957)

Russo, Vito. *The Celluloid Closet* (Harper and Row, 1987)

Sherriff, R. C. *No Leading Lady* (London: Victor Gollancz, 1968)

Skal, David J. *The Monster Show* (Plexus Publishing, 1994)

Index